# Rationalist Spirituality

An exploration of the meaning
of life and existence informed
by logic and science

# Rationalist Spirituality

An exploration of the meaning
of life and existence informed
by logic and science

Bernardo Kastrup

**BOOKS**

Winchester, UK
Washington, USA

First published by iff Books, 2011
iff Books is an imprint of John Hunt Publishing Ltd., No. 3 East Street, Alresford,
Hampshire SO24 9EE, UK
office1@jhpbooks.net
www.johnhuntpublishing.com
www.iff-books.com

For distributor details and how to order please visit the 'Ordering' section on our website.

Text copyright: 2009, 2010, 2017 by Bernardo Kastrup

ISBN: 978 1 84694 407 9
978 1 84694 735 3 (ebook)

A CIP catalogue record for this book is available from the British Library.

Design: Stuart Davies

UK: Printed and bound by CPI Group (UK) Ltd, Croydon, CR0 4YY
US: Printed and bound by Thomson Shore, 7300 West Joy Road, Dexter, MI 48130

We operate a distinctive and ethical publishing philosophy in
all areas of our business, from our global network of authors to
production and worldwide distribution.

# Contents

# Other books by Bernardo Kastrup

*Dreamed up Reality:*
*Diving into mind to uncover the astonishing hidden tale of nature*

*Meaning in Absurdity:*
*What bizarre phenomena can tell us about the nature of reality*

*Why Materialism Is Baloney:*
*How true skeptics know there is no death and fathom answers to life, the universe, and everything*

*Brief Peeks Beyond:*
*Critical essays on metaphysics, neuroscience, free will, skepticism and culture*

*More Than Allegory:*
*On religious myth, truth and belief*

Coming March 2019
*The Idea of the World:*
*A multi-disciplinary argument for the mental nature of reality*

To all conscious entities who have already contributed to the
unfinished set of subjective experiences I call my life...
...particularly Natalia Vorontsova.

# Chapter 1

# The hypothesis of meaning

The intuitive notion of meaning as an ultimate purpose for existence and life is deeply ingrained in the minds of most individuals. "Why am I here?" we ask ourselves. But a more fundamental question may be whether it makes any sense to ask about meaning in the first place. Nobel-laureate physicist Richard Feynman once said: "There are many things I don't know anything about, such as whether it means anything to ask why we're here, and what the question might mean."[1] Perhaps the very concept of meaning is fallacious; an illusion engendered by our brains, maybe as a consequence of a survival advantage in our evolution as a species.

As this book was being written, Matthew Hurley, Reginald Adams Jr. and Daniel Dennett were working on an evolutionary explanation for—of all things—our sense of humor. Humor seems to be such an abstract feeling, so removed from the framework of survival of the fittest, that any attempt to explain it through evolutionary biology may appear futile. Yet, in a talk, Daniel Dennett has suggested that humor is merely "a neural system wired up to reward the brain for doing a grubby clerical job."[2] If this is true, then it is not unreasonable that natural selection could have favored the survival of individuals with a more developed sense of humor. The validity of this theory aside, the fact is that serious philosophers can rationally argue that some of the most abstract of our feelings and motivations may actually have had very practical, survival-oriented applications during our evolutionary history. This alone should make us treat the question of meaning with caution.

Even if meaning is not merely an illusion, even if it truly exists in nature and it is a valid line of rational inquiry to search for it, there is no guarantee that we are intellectually equipped to grasp it. Logically, it is a possibility that the limitations of our own perception and comprehension may inherently prevent us from ever understanding the ultimate purpose of existence. In this case, as far as we are concerned, searching for meaning would be as futile as if the concept of meaning itself were fallacious.

Since you are reading this book, it is relatively safe to assume that you feel an intuitive drive for the search of meaning—or ultimate purpose—in your life. Nonetheless, the two scenarios described above may make you feel insecure about the validity of your own motivations. I wish I could give you a conclusive logical argument right here to convince you that meaning must be real and that it must be within the scope of our comprehension to grasp it. However, I cannot. What I can tell you is this: having meditated intensely on this for many years, from both sides of the argument, I have concluded to my own satisfaction that *there is indeed* meaning to existence.

So my invitation to you is this: assume, as starting hypotheses, that there is meaning in our lives and that it can be at least partially understood; what might that meaning then actually be? This book tries to sketch a rational answer to this question. Notice that I am not asking you to believe in these hypotheses blindly, but simply to keep an open mind about the possibility of their being true, so that we can pursue certain avenues of rational exploration. Then, after having read this book, you will be able to consider the answers we will arrive at and judge whether they make sense. Informed by this judgment, you will be able to look back and reconsider whether the concept of meaning is real or merely an illusion concocted by our brains.

## Chapter 2

# A search for ultimate purpose

"What happens but once ... might as well not have happened at all. If we have only one life to live, we might as well not have lived at all."[1] So does world-renowned author Milan Kundera capture the apparent futility of existence and its ephemeral character. If, as indicated by the second law of thermodynamics, all dynamic and organized structures in the universe, amongst which galaxies, stars and living creatures like you and me, will eventually expire without a trace, existence appears devoid of meaning. From the point of view of orthodox materialist science, all choices we make and experiences we live throughout our lives will, in time, be of no consequence. As such, our lives are light in their insignificance. Such "unbearable lightness of being," captured so powerfully in Kundera's work, is an agonizing and profoundly counter-intuitive perspective for many of us.

As rich and satisfying as our lives may sometimes be, most of us are marked by past or present experiences of profound pain and suffering. Loss, disappointment, frustration, anxiety, regret are familiar concepts to most of us. Is there anything we suffer for? And even when everything seems to go well in our lives, we sometimes cannot help but wonder whether there is any meaning in that either. What can be the meaning of our success, our material wealth, of our fleeting moments of happiness and even of our most profound rejoicing when, *given enough time*, not a trace or even a memory of our existence will be left behind? From a rational perspective, *can there be anything that survives our participation in the universe, adding something to its very essence in a way that transcends time?* Without it, there can be no true meaning to the dance of existence.

There are no obvious answers to this question. Yes, our

children survive us. The work we carry out during our lives often survives us too, be it through material entities like the buildings of an architect or more abstract entities like the ideas of a philosopher. But notice, the common thread behind these tentative answers is always the same: whatever outcome of our lives survives us, it only has meaning *through* the lives of other people like ourselves. The achievement of meaning is merely postponed in a self-similar way. After all, your children are people like you. The house built by the architect is only meaningful through the people who will live in it. The ideas left behind by the philosopher are only meaningful through the people who will read his books. But what, then, is the meaning of the lives of *those* people? If *their* lives are meaningless, so has the life of the philosopher been, for the meaning of his life seems to be conditional to that of theirs. This is an endless recursion. If the meaning of your life is the lives of your children, and the meaning of their lives are the lives of their children, and so on, where is the final meaning of it all that confers ultimate purpose to the lives of all previous generations of humans, and of human ancestors, all the way back to the beginning of time? In mathematics, a recursion cannot complete until a base-case, or termination condition, is reached. Recursions without a base-case continue on forever and are pointless, just like a computer program that does nothing but call itself repeatedly, never producing a result.

It could be that meaning is only realized at the base-case of one such a recursive process. In this case, the meaning of our lives would operate solely through the contributions we make to the lives of the people who survive our own existence, up until a point where the existence of a generation of living beings, perhaps in an unimaginably distant future, will serve an ultimate purpose in itself. Alternatively—or complementarily—it could be that our lives, ephemeral as they are, somehow have meaning in and by themselves, grounded in the present of our existence.

In the coming chapters, we will explore both alternatives. If, at the end of this exploration, we find no sound base-case for a recursive process of meaning, nor any anchor to ground meaning in the present of our existence, we may be left with the possibility that meaning is either merely an illusion or an unknowable truth. If instead—as I hope to show—there are reasonable ideas and lines of reasoning to substantiate the notion that there is indeed meaning to existence, and that such meaning can be at least intuited, then perhaps the lightness of our being is not at all unbearable. Perhaps the existence of the universe, and of our lives within it, is rich in meaning, significance and purpose. Perhaps it is precisely the perception of futility and inconsequence that has all along been an illusion of our minds. In this latter case, we will also need to suggest logical and rational mechanisms for the emergence of such an illusion in a universe that is, as hypothesized, rich in meaning. This is the journey of this book.

As a final note in this chapter, it should be clear that, when I talk of meaning, I refer to an ultimate purpose for the very existence of the universe, defined as the collection of all existing aspects of nature, known and unknown. I do not mean to imply an anthropomorphic purpose to particular local processes taking place within the universe, such as, for instance, evolution by natural selection. This way, the ideas in this book are agnostic of whether the evolution of the species has an intelligent causal agency or is driven by unintelligent, purely algorithmic processes. Even if we assume the latter viewpoint, there is still a valid question regarding the ultimate existential purpose of the underlying vehicles of the evolutionary process. In other words, even if evolution is the result of mechanical, algorithmic processes operating on a bio-molecular medium, why does that medium, and the natural laws operating on it, exist in the first place?

## Chapter 3

# A process of universal enrichment

Most religions are grounded in the concept of a Supreme Being that is perfect in Itself. Because there is a natural tendency in many of us to associate the idea of completeness to that of perfection, we then automatically envision a *perfect* Supreme Being as something that is also *complete*; that is, a Being to which nothing can be added. Although such an association between perfection and completeness is natural for most of us, depending on how it is interpreted it may seem to preempt the possibility of there being ultimate purpose to the universe's very existence. An entity that is complete, in the sense that nothing could possibly be added to it that was not already in it, *could not possibly have any purpose*. Think about this last statement for a moment, for the physical space it occupies on this page is overwhelmingly out of proportion with its importance. *Completeness is incompatible with purpose.*

A universe that comprises a complete entity is itself complete.[1] Indeed, the existence of a complete entity, as part of nature or as nature itself, logically implies the completeness of the whole of existence. And in a complete universe, the drama of our lives could not possibly add anything to the universe that were not already somewhere in it. The collection of human experience would be inconsequential.

If the universe were complete, wherever it 'needed to go,' it would already be there; whatever it needed to do, it would have already done it; whatever it needed to be, it would have already become it. Existence in a complete universe would be pure static being, if such a thing can even be conceived of. Completeness is incompatible with movement, yet it is beyond doubt that the universe is dynamic; it is certainly doing something, 'going somewhere,' and all of our empirical observations as conscious beings tell us that. Therefore, at some level, in some way, if there is purpose to existence the universe must *not* be complete.

Notice that, above, I deliberately distinguished the concept of completeness from that of perfection. Indeed, perhaps counter-intuitively, universal perfection is a relative concept conditional to subjective criteria; what is perfect for me might not be perfect for you. On the other hand, universal completeness can be defined as an absolute concept. Indeed, we can define completeness by saying that the universe will be complete *when its inherent potentials are fully realized.* Such statement does not depend on subjective criteria. Let us elaborate on why this is a reasonable statement to make.

We can logically conceive of things, phenomena or ideas that may exist in the universe even though we do not know them. These are already realized potentials of the universe that we may simply not have encountered yet. We can also logically conceive of things, phenomena or ideas that could potentially exist in the universe, but currently do not. These are then the unrealized potentials of the universe that render it incomplete. Indeed, it would be incoherent to consider the universe complete when aspects of its own inherent potential are not realized. So the definition of universal completeness above is reasonable and semantically consistent, albeit broad to the point of not being very useful. In subsequent chapters, I will attempt to define the notion of inherent potential more specifically, so to narrow down the scope of our definition of universal completeness.

For now, the point I want to make is that the universe can conceivably be perfect *and* incomplete concurrently. This would be the case if only a yet non-realized aspect of its own potential could, in principle, be brought into full realization through the operation of a process of enrichment. In this hypothetical case, the universe could be regarded as perfect precisely for being *in*complete. It would be this very incompleteness that leaves room for a dynamic process of enrichment, the dynamics of which may embody a subjective set of values associated with the idea of perfection. In other words, if a perfect universe is one that is dynamic in nature, one where there is movement, then such a perfect universe is necessarily incomplete.

It is intuitively appealing to think of the ultimate purpose of existence as the enrichment of the universe itself. However, it is impossible to even begin thinking about this idea rationally before we specify more strictly what is meant by enrichment; that is, until we say what enrichment is and—even more importantly—what it is not. And even once this is achieved, we will still be left with the burden to show that there is room for such an enrichment process in the universe without violating reason or our current scientific knowledge.

# Chapter 4

# The unrealized potential of consciousness

Your own consciousness is the most basic and familiar fact of your life. Indeed, in a sense it is the only fact, everything else being just subjective objects experienced in your consciousness. There are different definitions of consciousness but, in this book, I will consistently use the one philosophers call 'phenomenal consciousness': the substrate of subjective experience, such as the experience of hearing a sound, of seeing the redness of the color red, of feeling sad, etc. *If an entity is conscious, it means that there is something, anything, it is like to be this entity.* In other words, a conscious entity is capable of subjective experience. From this point on, every time I use the word 'consciousness' I will mean phenomenal consciousness, as defined above.

There is a distinction between a subjective experience and the neural correlates of such experience in the brain. For instance, our eyes are capable of detecting certain frequencies of electromagnetic radiation and of sending associated electrochemical signals for processing in the brain. Our subjective experience of that process may be described as 'seeing the color red.' However, all processes involved in detecting the corresponding electromagnetic radiation and processing the associated neural signals could, in principle, happen without any subjective experience accompanying them. As a matter of fact, much of the brain's neural activity escapes our ability to become explicitly aware of through introspection.[1] Why not all of it? After all, we could conceivably explain all form, structure and function in the universe—including human beings and their behavior—without any need for the existence of subjective experience.

Nothing that we know scientifically today satisfactorily

explains why or how subjective experience arises. This is often called the 'explanatory gap' or the 'hard problem of consciousness.' In his book *The Conscious Mind* philosopher David Chalmers has elaborated extensively on this notion.[2] Joseph Levine has also offered solid arguments illustrating the gap.[3] Technical discussions about the explanatory gap still go on today in philosophical circles. However, for our purposes in this book the important message is this: *as far as consciousness is concerned, science provides an incomplete model of nature.* In fact, all we have determined scientifically is that there are neural correlates of objects in consciousness.[4] In other words, we know that the perceptions and thoughts that we are aware of occur together with specific excitations of associated brain structures.

The explanatory gap and the definition of consciousness given above will become clearer if we contrast them with a common intuition we have about the *lack* of consciousness. Whether the intuition itself is correct or not, it exists and is strong, so I will use it. Consider your personal computer: it is capable of highly sophisticated and adaptive behavior; it performs complex and varied functions; it responds to your commands and to data it receives from other means, like the Internet. However, most people would assume that there is nothing it is like to *be* a computer. In other words, most people do not believe that a computer feels anything, in the broadest sense of the word; that a computer is capable of subjective experience or inner life; that the calculations it performs are somehow objects of inner experience. For most people, a computer performs all of its tasks 'in the dark,' in a mechanical manner, not very different in nature, but only in scale and complexity, from an old abacus. Whereas we can make an analogy between the calculations taking place inside the computer and the neural correlates of consciousness taking place inside the brain, it seems clear that the computer does not *experience* those calculations the way we experience the neural processing in our brain. In fact, even if we imagine computers becoming increasingly more sophisticated and performing increasingly more complicated tasks that eventually become comparable in complexity to our own brain processing, there appears to be something very fundamental and intrinsic about the mechanical nature of computers that renders them incapable of subjective experience. It is *that* intuited difference between you and a computer that characterizes consciousness.

With the growing relevance of the complexity sciences in recent times, a speculative, purely materialist view of consciousness has emerged. Proponents of this view argue that, although individual neurons and relatively small systems of interconnected neurons are akin to computers and do not have consciousness, if the complexity of the system is increased with the addition of more and more interconnected neurons, there will be a point where the system as a whole will somehow become conscious. Consciousness is then seen as an *emergent property* of a *sufficiently complex* system exhibiting a *particular structure*. Nobody knows what this structure is or what level of complexity is complex enough. The problem with this argument is that it requires the appearance of a new property in a system that is not explainable by, nor related to, the properties of the added components of the system. Indeed, the idea of a computer suddenly becoming conscious at the moment enough processors have been added to it is akin to the idea of a stereo turning into a TV set when enough speakers are connected to it; or that of getting a motorbike to fly by equipping it with a bigger engine. In the same way that more speakers affect the properties of a stereo in a manner that is totally unrelated to the property of displaying images, so the simple addition of more neurons must affect the properties of the physical brain in a manner that is unrelated to the property of being conscious.

A vocal proponent of the view that consciousness is an emergent property of sufficiently complex material systems is the inventor and futurologist Ray Kurzweil.[5] In a debate

11

between Kurzweil and Yale University professor David Gelernter in 2006, Gelernter countered Kurzweil's view on consciousness by stating that "it's not enough to say [that consciousness is] an emergent phenomenon. Granted, but how? How does it work? Unless those questions are answered, we don't understand the human mind."[6] Gelernter chose the most basic and straight-forward way to counter Kurzweil's position. Today, the materialist argument that consciousness is simply an emergent property of complex material systems cannot be substantiated. It is an appeal to magic rather than an argument. Therefore, we remain with the explanatory gap: nothing that we know scientifically today satisfactorily explains why or how subjective experience arises.

An easy thought experiment to help you gain some intuition about the explanatory gap is this: imagine a hypothetical universe identical to ours in every way except in that consciousness does not exist in it. In this hypothetical universe, none of our current scientific models of nature and its laws would break down. In fact, a universe without consciousness is entirely consistent with all of our current scientific models. However, if you did the same exercise with any other known property of nature, be it a fundamental property like mass or an emergent property like chaotic system behavior, many of our scientific models would need to be revised. So clearly there is something missing in our understanding of nature as far as consciousness is concerned. The explanatory gap is real.

In the thought experiment above, the hypothetical universe must be identical to ours in all observable ways, including the presence of people in it. People in this hypothetical universe would be indistinguishable from people in our own universe, as far as you could observe from the outside. However, from the inside, there would be nothing it is like to *be* those people. They would be like mechanical zombies, lacking consciousness entirely. As a matter of fact, those zombies would claim to be conscious. They would report on love, pain and all conscious experiences familiar to you, but they would do it as highly sophisticated biological computers programmed to do so under certain circumstances. The point of the thought experiment, imagined this way, is to highlight that science could conceivably explain all structure and behavior, as manifested by people when observed from the outside, but it fundamentally says nothing about the subjective experience of *being* a conscious person. Indeed, the form and behavior of the zombies in our hypothetical universe would remain entirely consistent with all of our science, and science does not make statements about anything beyond that.

Everything that anyone has ever experienced — including all joy, suffering, insight, awe, etc. — has always been subjective objects in consciousness. We reasonably postulate the existence of an objective world outside consciousness but, strictly speaking, this is an assumption. In his *Discourse on the Method*, René Descartes introduced the idea that the only thing whose existence we can be absolutely certain of is our own consciousness. He captured it in his now famous dictum *"cogito ergo sum"* ("I think, therefore I am"). Beyond that, we only have access to what comes to us through our five senses and cannot ascertain its objective reality without doubt. As brain scientist Dr. Andrew Newberg put it, "The most basic question is what is the fundamental nature of reality and how do we come to experience it. The problem is that we have a block between how we perceive the world and how the world really is. We're trapped by our brain, by our inability to go beyond thinking and perception."[7] This notion is taken to an extreme in the philosophical position of solipsism, the idea that one's own mind is all that exists. While I do not endorse solipsism, I do think that the rationale behind it gives us a valid perspective regarding the primacy of consciousness in our perception of reality.

During the normal operation of our brains, inputs from our

sensory organs are processed by complex networks of connected neurons, leading to neural correlates of objects in consciousness. Since—at least in regular states of consciousness—we have no direct access to an objective truth outside our individual minds, we assume that the neural correlates of consciousness correctly mirror an external reality that exists independently of ourselves. We do that by comparing our conscious perceptions with what other individuals, themselves assumed to be conscious, report about their conscious perceptions. It is the overwhelming consistency among these reports that cements in our minds the conviction that there exists an objective world we live in.

For instance, if I stand on a beach watching the waves and people around me report that they are watching waves as well, I must then very reasonably assume that there are indeed waves out there, even though I have no direct way to ascertain it. You may argue that I could jump into the ocean and come in direct contact with the waves, but all that would accomplish is to expose *additional* ones of my five senses to the water, like my sense of touch. All contact I would have with the assumed truth of objective waves 'out there' would still be through the electrochemical signals that my sensory organs send to my brain, thereby producing neural correlates of objects in consciousness.

In a sense, your entire world is locked up in your head. The example above may sound forced and artificial to you, as an adult whose brain is already wired with established models of reality, but things would be a lot less obvious to an infant growing up. It is only over time that our brains wire up mental models to accommodate the objects and behaviors that are consistently experienced by ourselves and reported by others. We will explore this in a lot more detail in subsequent chapters.

As discussed above, although reasonable assumptions can be made about a world outside ourselves, ultimately all of our perceptions and thoughts exist only as objects in our consciousness. Whereas solipsism is an unreasonable position to take, given the overwhelming consistency of reports from different individuals about the world they perceive, we must be cautious about attributing unreserved ontological truth to certain assumed properties of this world, for we do not have direct access to it. This way, as far as we as conscious beings are concerned, consciousness is the sole ground of existence. A universe without consciousness would be like a concert without an audience: Could the orchestra even be said to play if there is nobody listening? As a matter of fact, this is a question that modern science has addressed.

Quantum mechanics, the most accurate scientific theory ever devised by humankind, is a model of nature wherein two fundamental processes can be found at work. The first process is a linear, deterministic process described by the so-called 'Schrödinger's equation.' All you need to know about it, for the purposes of our argumentation, is that Schrödinger's equation describes an envelope of possibilities—potential realities—called a 'wave function.' This envelope changes over time, propagating like a wave in a very predictable way. At any moment in time, armed with the correct wave function, we could in principle determine what the possible 'realities' of that moment are. However, the wave function does not determine which of the possible realities actually manifests; it just tells us what the alternatives are in potentiality. In other words, the wave function does not describe reality as we consciously observe it, but simply establishes boundaries on what can potentially be observed.

The second fundamental process of quantum mechanics is an apparent collapse of the wave function. It is through this apparent collapse that the envelope of possible realities turns into a specific manifested reality. This is not a deterministic process, in the sense that there is no way, even in principle, to exactly predict which of the possible realities actually manifests to our observation upon apparent collapse. All we can experience as conscious beings is the non-deterministic reality emerging from an apparently collapsed wave function. Everything else within the original envelope of possibilities described by the wave function will have been just alternatives that never came into existence in our physical universe.

The above is an accepted idea in orthodox science, but it can be *interpreted* in different ways. Two general interpretations of quantum mechanics are popular today, as discussed by physicist Erich Joos.[8] The first is the so-called 'many-worlds' interpretation, attributed to physicist Hugh Everett III. According to this interpretation, the collapse of the wave function is not real, but merely an illusion. All possible realities comprised in the wave function actually manifest physically, but each in a different parallel universe. This way, our universe is thought to be constantly 'branching out,' like a tree, into different versions of itself, each manifesting a different one of the possibilities of each moment. Since we ourselves are part of reality, multiple versions of ourselves are postulated to occupy different parallel universes. The memories you hold right now reflect the path this version of you took along the different branches of the tree. For instance, in the branch of the tree you occupy right now, you have picked up this book and are now reading it. In a different branch of the tree, in a parallel universe, another version of you is doing something else right now, with no memory of having picked up this book.

If you are not a physicist, your first impulse may be to discount the many-worlds interpretation as laughable. This would be understandable but unwarranted. Indeed, starting from the mathematical framework we know to be true, 'many-worlds' seems to be the interpretation that follows in the most direct way. However, from a scientific perspective, the main problem with the many-worlds interpretation is the lack of *parsimony*. An accepted rule-of-thumb in science is that a good theory is one that requires the least complex explanation for an observed phenomenon. The many-worlds interpretation, from a certain point of view, proposes the most complex explanation of nature that can be conceived; namely, that everything that could possibly happen actually does.

The appeal of the many-worlds interpretation to orthodox physics is its role in preserving a form of deterministic thinking, a core value of orthodox science. A deterministic universe is one where the present and future would have been entirely determined at the moment of creation. To be a little more formal about what I mean, a deterministic universe is such that all its future states could be, in principle, exactly calculated from a complete knowledge of the universe's present state and its laws. In such a universe, everything you think, every decision you believe to make, everything you experience, would be the inescapable consequences of a predictable interplay of subatomic particles. The universe, and everything that happens within it, would be predetermined the same way that the trajectories of balls in a billiard game are entirely pre-determined at the moment the cue stick hits the cue ball. But quantum wave function collapse violates determinism, since the reality that actually materializes at each moment cannot be predicted even in principle.

With the many-worlds interpretation, however, there is no actual wave function collapse but just an *appearance* of collapse from the point of view of an observer traversing particular branches of the tree of splitting universes. By postulating that every possible outcome predictably does happen — though in different and mutually inaccessible parallel universes — the many-worlds interpretation rescues a form of literal determinism, albeit defeating the spirit of determinism. The price to pay for this precarious rescue is the most dramatic departure conceivable from another core value of science: parsimony.

The other plausible interpretation of quantum mechanics is that some form of collapse does take place, in the sense that the material world assumes only one of the many possible configurations entailed by the wave function. To this day, it is a mystery what the causal agency of wave function collapse is. Indeed, since no material reality manifests until *after* collapse takes place, it seems that whatever causes collapse must come from *outside* material reality. This is what led renowned mathematician John van Neumann, Nobel-laureate physicist Eugene Wigner and many others to postulate consciousness as the causal agency of wave function collapse. After all, as we have seen when discussing the explanatory gap, consciousness has an immaterial quality that seems utterly unrelated to the properties of matter. Actually, consciousness is the *only* fact of nature we know of that has this immaterial quality. It seems to be the only obvious, observable (at least from within) fact of nature that remains outside the scope of our scientific models, including quantum models themselves. As such, *it could hypothetically cause wave function collapse from outside the material aspects reality.*

This interpretation of quantum mechanics is often referred to as 'Wigner's interpretation.' According to it, without conscious observation the entire universe would be just an amorphous realm of possibilities with no material reality. Things only 'pop' into material existence upon an observation by a conscious observer. Therefore, still according to this interpretation, the world 'out there' depends upon objects in consciousness 'in here' for its existence. Interpretations of quantum mechanics that consider wave function collapse to be in some way real recognize a single universe. However, they require us to part with the notion that such single universe is deterministic.

Today, there is little scientific basis to decide between the many-worlds, Wigner's, and even a few other interpretations of quantum mechanics. So we have a choice. My own choice is Wigner's interpretation that consciousness causes some form of wave function collapse. I believe it to be the most natural, simple and logical interpretation of what we observe in experiments. The only other serious contender — the many-worlds interpretation — is unreasonably inflationary in my view. Moreover, the main counter-argument used against Wigner's interpretation is that it is somehow unreasonable to imagine that consciousness can play any causal role in determining external reality. To me, this is simply a prejudice that reflects a natural inertia in replacing an age-old thought framework with a new one, but has no logical or empirical basis beyond that. On the basis of everything we know today, there is nothing unreasonable about inferring that consciousness plays an on-going role in determining reality. Indeed, with Wigner's interpretation, such an inference is possible without violating reason or the known laws of physics.

From two different perspectives—namely, a philosophical hypothesis derived from the science of perception and an interpretation of quantum mechanics—consciousness seems to play a primary role in determining what happens in reality. A universe without consciousness would be like a stage play without an audience. Philosophically, we cannot say that the stage play exists when not correlated with objects in consciousness. Physically, Wigner's interpretation states that, without a conscious audience, the stage play would forever remain in an amorphous realm of possibilities outside material reality.

*Such primacy of consciousness in grounding existence allows us to infer that a process of universal enrichment, as postulated in the previous chapter, should be a process of consciousness enrichment.* Under this framework, the as-of-yet unrealized potential of the incomplete universe is the degree, reach or quality of consciousness in it. If this is correct, then the meaning of existence—its ultimate purpose—is an enrichment of consciousness.

## Chapter 5

# The brain as a consciousness transceiver

There is a clear relationship between consciousness and the brain. Scientific analysis has shown significant correlation between objects in consciousness and specific neural activation patterns in the brain.[1] We also know that electromagnetic stimulation of the brain leads to alteration of subjective experiences.[2] In addition, from direct personal experience, many of us are familiar with the effects that alcohol and other drugs can have in our states of consciousness through affecting the biochemistry of the brain. Finally, we all know that sufficient damage to the brain, or the use of anesthetics,[3] consistently leads to an apparent loss of consciousness (or at least to the loss of a memory of consciousness). Therefore, we can say that a functioning physical brain is a *necessary* condition for the manifestation of our *regular* states of consciousness. The question of whether or not it is a *sufficient* condition is another matter.

From that perspective, one of the problems with Wigner's interpretation of quantum mechanics is this: if our regular consciousness causes collapse of the wave function, thereby manifesting physical reality, then who or what causes the reality of the physical brain, a necessary condition for the manifestation of regular consciousness in the first place? After all, the physical brain, as any physical structure, must obey the same laws as the rest of physical reality. Its wave function must be collapsed for it to exist in the material world. We have thus a chicken-and-egg problem that needs resolving.

To motivate Wigner's interpretation of quantum mechanics, we stated that wave function collapse needed a causal agency from outside material reality. Then, we postulated consciousness as a natural candidate for that. This implies that consciousness somehow transcends physical reality and is at least not entirely governed by the known laws of quantum mechanics. To resolve the chicken-and-egg problem associated with Wigner's interpretation we can thus imagine the following: the physical brain is both the *result* of an initial manifestation of consciousness in the physical world *and* its necessary *platform* for further interacting with material reality on a regular basis. In other words, the organic growth of a biological nervous system is what happens in the material world when consciousness begins to penetrate it. As such, it is *consciousness itself* that causes the series of collapses of the growing brain's wave function entailed by its development. Consciousness *builds* the brain, so the speak, for later use. Then, once completed, the nervous system acts as the necessary stage and interface from which consciousness can more extensively interact with the physical world at large, which explains the correlations between brain states and subjective experience (this will be discussed in more details shortly). The growth and ongoing life of a biological nervous system can thus be regarded as the formation and maintenance, respectively, of a necessary interface between consciousness and the physical world, for the regular manifestation of consciousness in the physical world. But consciousness performs this formation and maintenance from *outside* the physical world.

The line of argument above may suggest some form of substance dualism; that is, the idea that consciousness and the physical world, including the brain itself, are made of different 'stuff.' However, this would be incompatible with the discussion in Chapter 4, in which we concluded not only that consciousness is primary, but that we cannot be at all sure that there exists anything outside or independent of consciousness. We can reconcile these threads of argument by imagining that the known physical or material world must somehow arise from, and be 'made of,' a *trans*personal part of consciousness that extends far beyond our individual awareness. This way, consciousness is the sole 'substance' of all existence.

Now, because that transpersonal part of consciousness obviously escapes the range of our introspection, we may call it the 'obfuscated mind.' Thus, according to this view, physical or material reality is an experiential manifestation of the obfuscated mind, triggered by our interaction with it through (quantum mechanical) observation. As such, there is indeed a form of dualism between our personal, self-reflective awareness (which I shall continue to refer to simply as 'consciousness') on the one hand, and physical or material reality as a manifestation of the transpersonal obfuscated mind on the other, even though the 'substance' at play in both cases is the same. It is in this specific sense, and this sense alone, that I will continue to allude to a form of mind/body dualism in the remainder of this book.

In order to continue our analysis, we need a framework to construe how consciousness interacts with the material aspects of reality. Since we concluded earlier that a physical brain is a necessary condition for this, we can then regard the brain as a 'transceiver' of consciousness in the material world; that is, a kind of 'telephone.' The word 'transceiver' is an amalgamation of 'transmitter' and 'receiver,' suggesting a kind of two-way communication between consciousness and the physical world.

To gain some intuition about the logic of this model, consider robotic interplanetary exploration vehicles like NASA's Mars rovers *Spirit* and *Opportunity*.[4] The rovers were launched in 2003 and spent years exploring the surface of Mars with cameras and other scientific instruments. Despite being controlled remotely from Earth, the robotic vehicles had a certain degree of autonomy embodied in their on-board navigation, data processing and housekeeping algorithms. Beyond this, they operated as transceiver platforms for the humans on Earth. All images mission control could see of Mars were captured and transmitted by the robotic vehicles. All activities that mission control wanted to carry out on Mars—like drilling on rocks, taking pictures or moving around—were executed by the robotic vehicles after receiving commands from Earth. In a sense, the members of mission control were very much present on Mars, interacting with the Martian environment through a number of sensors and actuators. Not only was information collected, but concrete changes were also left on Mars as a result of their presence there, like tracks on soil or holes in rocks. However, their presence on Mars was a virtual one, operating through the transceiver platforms constituted by the robotic vehicles.

By now, as a critical reader, you will have already understood where I am going with this and will be asking yourself: "Why would nature impose on itself such limitations as the ones faced by interplanetary explorers operating robotic vehicles?" It apparently makes no sense and sounds utterly forced and artificial. Nonetheless, I have come to conclude that it is the answer to this very question that lies at the heart of the meaning of existence and, as a consequence, the meaning of life. But let us not rush. We will address this question head-on in the coming chapters. For now, I ask for your patience and an open mind. All we are trying to accomplish in this chapter is to postulate the simplest possible model for the interaction of consciousness with the material world that simultaneously satisfies the two conditions identified earlier: first, that consciousness transcends the domain of quantum mechanics; and second, that the physical brain is a necessary condition for the regular manifestation of consciousness in material reality. The first condition is motivated by Wigner's interpretation of quantum mechanics, whereas the second condition is motivated by empirical observations of the relationship between brain function and states of consciousness.

Continuing on with our analogy, mission control on Earth was limited in their ability to receive information from Mars, as well as to send commands to Mars, by the capabilities of the robotic vehicles physically on Mars. They could not carry out any activity on Mars that was not supported by the on-board instruments and actuators of the robots. They also could not receive any information from Mars whose acquisition was not supported by the capabilities of the on-board sensors and information processing devices of the robots. Another main limitation was the communication bandwidth between mission control on Earth and the robotic vehicles on Mars. In other words, the amount of information per second that could be transmitted back and forth between Earth and Mars limited what could be accomplished. A way around bandwidth limitations was to perform as much data processing in the robots themselves as possible. It was much more efficient to transmit 'pre-digested' data from Mars to Earth—in the form of experimental results or compressed images, for instance—than raw data. Indeed, raw data tends to require orders of magnitude more communication bandwidth than processed data. Therefore, the robotic vehicles carried out as much data analysis as possible locally, on Mars, before transmitting 'pre-digested' results back to earth. The same holds the other way around: the more autonomy the on-board robotic systems had in terms of taking their own decisions about routes to take or things to do, the less raw commands needed to be sent out from Earth. Ideally, only exploration objectives would be sent out from Earth, the robots themselves determining how to go about achieving those pre-set objectives. For instance, it would be much more efficient to send a command in the form of "Find your way to point A," instead of "Drive one meter forward; then stop; then turn 45 degrees; then drive another five meters forward; then stop," etc. Naturally, the former alternative would require a higher degree of autonomy and, dare I say, *intelligence* on-board the robotic transceiver platform. We will discuss more about the role of intelligence with respect to consciousness in Chapter 7. For now, bear with me a little longer.

It is conceivable that advanced robotic explorers in the future will go beyond 'pre-digesting' data and use their artificial intelligence systems to already compute entire sets of data interpretations and conclusions locally, thereafter sending to Earth only those conclusions. Mission control on Earth would then never get access to the original data collected, but *only to the interpretation of the data* as developed by the robots themselves. Mission control's understanding of another planet would, in this case, be restricted to the robot's own ability to model and interpret the data it collects from that planet.

Our physical brain is an amazing information processing platform. It receives information from our five senses, processes and analyzes it, and issues commands to the rest of our physical body. In the framework of orthodox science, this is in every way analogous to advanced interplanetary robotic explorers, except one: orthodox science postulates that the brain is the final arbiter. Here, instead, we are positing that the brain is a platform for acquiring data, processing it, analyzing it, transmitting the results of this analysis to consciousness, receiving causal influences from consciousness, further processing these causal influences, and finally issuing resulting commands to the rest of the physical body. If this sounds too far-fetched to you, bear with me a little longer, for soon we will look at specific physiological mechanisms in the brain that could support this. There are very reputable scientists out there who take this idea very seriously.

Most scientists feel comfortable with the idea of the brain crunching data before presenting it to consciousness. After all, this is pretty much consistent with all scientific data we have on perception. However, most are not comfortable with the idea that the brain also receives causal influences from an immaterial consciousness. The latter would be an instance of what is called 'downward causation' in philosophy.

Philosophically speaking, if immaterial consciousness could not make choices that influence our thoughts and actions in the world, our self-reflective selves would be mere spectators of the dance of existence. We would not be able to change the course of things in any way and free will would be merely an illusion. All of our thoughts and actions would be fully determined by the electrochemical processes of our brain physiology. Consciousness would be limited to observing but not influencing anything through choice. We would just *think* we are making decisions, but this in itself would be an artifact of our brain physiology and the way its operation is presented to consciousness.

Such a picture of reality could still be compatible with there being meaning to existence. After all, there would still be an audience to watch the stage play and confer on it its material existence through wave function collapse, even though the audience could not make choices about the turn of events in the play. There would still be self-reflective experience giving meaning to the universe, though that experience would not be able to causally affect the universe's dynamics. So we cannot discard this view as inconsistent with our starting hypotheses.

However, empirical observations tilt the balance in favor of downward causation. Indeed, important indications that consciousness causally influences brain function come from neuroscience experiments. Tests have been performed in which subjects were asked to direct their conscious attention in particular ways, driven by their own willpower. Brain scan analyses of the effects of such conscious effort revealed that the effort could physically alter neural circuitry and brain function, even in cases of brain pathology. This has been called 'self-directed neuroplasticity' and is an accepted phenomenon.[5] It suggests that consciousness—and choice as an object in consciousness—is in some sense separate from, yet can causally affect, brain function. Otherwise, how could something that is merely a result of brain activity choose to, and actually cause, a change in the very brain that generates it in the first place? That would be analogous to saying, for instance, that images of slides projected onto a screen could somehow choose and affect the inner-workings of the projector that generates them in the first place.

The more technically astute reader may argue that, if there were a built-in feedback mechanism in the brain whereby neural correlates of experience could physically influence neurophysiology, then self-directed neuroplasticity could be explained without contradiction with the hypothesis that consciousness is purely the result of brain activity. In our analogy, this would be like saying that the projector has a built-in digital camera focused on the images projected on the wall, and that the signals captured by the camera are wired directly into the inner mechanisms of the projector, thereby causally influencing its functionality.

Strictly speaking, there is nothing illogical about this possibility, though it would require a complex, global feedback mechanism in the brain that neuroscientists today could not begin to explain. Indeed, in some of the experiments performed, the subjects were instructed to use their willpower to alter the very emotional reaction that would be normally expected. For instance, when shown a photograph that would normally enact sexual arousal, subjects were instructed to use conscious effort to modify this instinctive, hardwired emotional response. Surprisingly enough, such efforts were often met with success. If conscious experiences were entirely the result of deterministic electrochemistry in the brain, the experience of sexual arousal should be a deterministic outcome. Yet, this does not appear to be the case. As Jeffrey Schwartz, of the UCLA Neuropsychiatric Institute, put it, "When, as happens in a growing number of studies, the subject makes an active response aimed at systematically altering the nature of the emotional reaction ... then the demand that the data be understood solely from the perspective of brain-based causal mechanisms is a severe and counter-intuitive constraint."[6]

This strongly suggests—though it admittedly does not prove—that consciousness is not simply a result of brain activity, but somehow is able to exert causal influences on the brain from 'outside' or 'above' the brain. Such downward causation performed by consciousness on brain structure and function, in turn, may influence what other subjective objects later appear in consciousness.

The orthodox position that consciousness is merely a result of brain activity rests, in a way, on the assumption that brain activity is deterministic. In other words, it assumes that the brain's structure and perceptual inputs fully determine conscious experience. However, if the outcomes of neural processing fundamentally depend on quantum mechanical principles, we have seen that brain activity then cannot be deterministic: it will depend on wave function collapse that is caused, according to Wigner's interpretation, by immaterial consciousness. The question now is: Do we have reason to believe that neural processing should be understood on the basis of quantum mechanics? It turns out that we do. And this offers even more evidence that, indeed, consciousness is not merely the result of brain function, but instead transcends the brain, causally influencing its function.

Mathematician and physicist Roger Penrose,[7] anesthesiologist Stuart Hameroff[8] and physicist Henry Stapp,[9] amongst others, have elaborated upon specific aspects of brain function that seem to be quantum mechanical in nature. In doing so, they have proposed different mechanisms for how immaterial consciousness could interact with the physical brain. These proposed mechanisms could satisfactorily explain self-directed neuroplasticity. Notice that the articulation in this book is agnostic of which particular mechanism of brain-consciousness interaction holds true, as long as we can reasonably infer that there is one such a mechanism consistent with the transceiver model described earlier. Henry Stapp's proposed mechanism is a particularly elegant and eloquent example, so I will describe it in a little more detail below to help you gain some intuition about how all this could work in the brain.

We know that the brain is composed of networks of interconnected, specialized information-processing cells called neurons. Neurons in the networks are connected to each other through nerve terminals, which can transmit signals across neurons. All brain function rests on signals communicated between neurons through these nerve terminals. Each time a neuron tries to communicate with another, this communication attempt is mediated by the movement of calcium ions inside the nerve terminals. Therefore, brain function dependents on whether or not the movement of these calcium ions triggers each attempted neural communication. Now here is the key: Stapp states that the movement of the calcium ions, given the dimensions and conditions involved, must happen in accordance with quantum mechanical laws. Consequently, whether or not the calcium ions trigger a communication between neurons is the result of wave function collapse, itself caused by immaterial consciousness. According to Stapp, this is how immaterial consciousness interacts with the physical brain. Notice that, with this mechanism, there is no discrete 'antenna' or localized region of the brain where the interaction with consciousness exclusively takes place. Instead, myriad nerve terminals distributed throughout the brain respond to the causal influences of immaterial consciousness. Without consciousness causing wave function collapse at the nerve terminals, all brain processing would grind to a halt, so to speak.

Still according to Stapp, it is consciousness that *chooses* whether any particular signal between two neurons actually gets across or not. Therefore, this model entails that neural processing is the result of quantum wave function collapse triggered, and chosen, by consciousness. This is literally downward causation, entailing the reception of causal influences from consciousness by the brain. So here we have a physiological structure to enable the 'receiver' part of our transceiver model of brain-consciousness interaction.

The chance of signals being exchanged among any particular subset of the brain's myriad neurons depends on their interconnect architecture. It must also obey the probability distribution entailed by Schrödinger's equation, irrespective of downward causation. In addition, signals from our senses feed this neural processing with raw data, influencing the possible configurations within the envelope of the wave function. Therefore, the material structure of the physical brain, the inputs from the sensory organs, and the external world that feeds the sensory organs with information, all impose stringent boundary constraints on the neural signal processing that can potentially take place in the brain. Consequently, consciousness is given only a well-defined and limited 'menu,' so to speak, of possible perceptions and alternatives for action that are determined by material structure. This entails the transmission of information from material reality to consciousness, tackling the 'transmitter' part of our transceiver model of brain-consciousness interaction.

We have now postulated a detailed mechanism for a two-way interaction between brain and consciousness that is analogous to how mission control operated on Mars through its robotic transceivers.

Notice that Stapp's model entails that consciousness not only causes wave function collapse, but is also the agency that *chooses* which of the possible realities within the envelope of the wave function actually materializes. Other authors have proposed different agencies of choice for wave function collapse in the physical brain. Mathematician Roger Penrose, for instance, has proposed an abstract world of platonic values as the agency of choice. However, Stapp's postulate that consciousness itself is the agency of choice is the model that requires the least number of assumptions for the thought-line of this book, so we will use it as our working hypothesis from this point on.

## Chapter 6

# Science does not claim to explain it all

We have now talked extensively about the role of consciousness in our perception of reality, such perception being the only reality we can know to exist. We have also talked about the causal role of consciousness in influencing neural processes in the physical brain. Finally, we have seen that consciousness cannot be explained in terms of physicality, therefore remaining a mystery as far as materialist science is concerned.

But have we not already measured, and can we not already explain, all phenomena through our materialist science? If we could, there would be no room for immaterial consciousness, nor would there be room for consciousness to play any causal or explanatory role. After all, everything is supposed to be explainable in terms of the position and momentum of subatomic particles. In other words, our 'theory of everything,' developed to model the behavior of nature at a microscopic level, should supposedly be sufficient to explain all macroscopic phenomena we observe, such as rocks, trees, brains, people and stars. This would leave immaterial consciousness out of the picture, as well as contradict our entire argument. More broadly, this would close the door on spirituality, for the core of spirituality is the notion that there is an aspect of reality that (a) is not physically determined and (b) plays a causal role in the material world.

The notion that science may obviate spirituality is tempting because our science and technology have been spectacularly successful in modeling and engineering nature. We have a natural bias to assume that, already today, science can explain the whole of nature in a causally-closed manner. In other words, we believe that science can so completely explain everything we observe that it leaves no room for other, yet unknown

31

explanations, influences or dynamics. We tend to think that, in our own plane of reality, everything has been satisfactorily explained and there is no room for anything immaterial.

However, this bias is not justifiable by the current status of scientific development. Not only do we know for sure that there is a lot we do not know, we also have not yet closed the gap between much of what we do know and the phenomena we observe. In other words, we have not yet fully explained the variety of observations we make—even the trivial, everyday ones—on the basis of the fundamental laws of physics we know to be true. We just *assume* that such explanations must exist and will lead to no surprises. It is outside the scope of this book to catalog all instances where our scientific knowledge is known to be incomplete but, to impress my point upon you, I will mention a few examples.

In the field of cosmology, observations of gravitational and acceleration effects on visible matter at a cosmological scale—such as stars and galaxies—have strongly indicated the presence of an extra type of 'matter' and an extra type of 'energy' in the universe that cannot be seen or detected by any direct means. Such 'extra' matter and energy came to be called 'dark matter' and 'dark energy,' respectively, because we cannot see them.[1] Today, we barely know how to think about dark energy and can only infer its existence from the accelerated rate at which galaxies move away from one another. Regarding dark matter, we know that it does not interact with the known electromagnetic spectrum. As such, it does not emit, absorb or reflect light, being entirely transparent. Clearly, it is not made of atoms.

An understanding of the nature of dark matter and of dark energy has remained elusive to science. In plain language, we do not know what the stuff is. What we do know from indirect measurements is that more than a staggering 95% of everything in the known universe seems to be dark matter or dark energy. In other words, we have very little idea about what more than

95% of the stuff out there actually is, but we know that it must be there.

Now, often people tend to assume that this dark matter is somewhere out there in interstellar space, far removed from our immediate environment. But scientists have reason to believe that we are actually immersed in the stuff. Huge amounts of dark matter may be filling the room where you are sitting right now, coming and going through walls and passing through your body. It is just that dark matter seems to be so non-interactive with normal matter that we cannot see, feel or even detect it with instruments through any direct means. Think about that for a moment.

Moving on to the field of physics, today we have a very successful model for the behavior of matter at microscopic scales, called the 'Standard Model' of particle physics. However, we have a very different model, called 'General Relativity,' to explain the behavior of matter at large interplanetary scales. These two models are sometimes known as the 'theory of the very small' and the 'theory of the very big.' Both are very accurate in their respective scales, but are very different. We cannot expect nature to simultaneously conform to two inconsistent sets of rules. Moreover, from the theory of the 'Big Bang' we know that the entire known universe was once compressed in a microscopic scale, so we cannot satisfactorily explain the universe's evolution from very small to very big unless we reconcile these two theories. If and when we finally succeed in such an endeavor, our understanding of physics may depart significantly from the framework we have today.

Attempts are now in the works to capture the essential dynamics of the 'theory of the very big' in new versions of the 'theory of the very small.' This way, science hopes to derive a 'theory of everything' at a microscopic level. With this microscopic 'theory of everything,' science hopes to explain all phenomena in the universe, even the very big ones, based on the properties and behavior of the smallest building blocks everything in the universe is assumed to be made of. As a taste of things to come, the latest attempts in this direction, like superstring theories and M-theory, seem to indicate that the universe has many more than the three dimensions of space and the one dimensional of time that we can observe.[2] In fact, M-theory suggests that the universe has eleven dimensions; that is a lot of room for properties and phenomena we cannot begin to intuit today.

In particle physics, relatively simple phenomena are studied in an attempt to model them at the most basic level of known nature: that of subatomic particles. In the field of biology, on the other hand, the level of complexity of the phenomena under study becomes so high that it is completely impractical to model them at the subatomic level. Scientists then operate on a higher level of abstraction: instead of taking subatomic particles as the underlying building blocks of bottom-up models, they directly model larger structures, such as cells and tissues, from top-down observation of their compound behavior and properties. We *assume* that the known laws of physics, demonstrated to hold at the subatomic level, are solely responsible for the observed behavior and properties of cells and tissues in a causally-closed manner. In other words, we assume that there is nothing about the properties and behavior of tissues and cells that cannot be explained in terms of the properties and behavior of subatomic particles. But today we cannot check this assumption because we do not have the capability to perform a subatomic-level simulation of a cell to compare to the observed behavior and properties of a real cell. So we just do not really know if everything we observe at a macroscopic level would turn out consistent with a 'theory of everything' derived from observations at the microscopic level. As acknowledged by Mile Gu and his collaborators, "The question of whether some macroscopic laws may be fundamental statements about nature or may be deduced from some 'theory of everything' remains a topic of debate among scientists."[3]

Indeed, if we start from our most fundamental, microscopic-level theories and associated equations, we cannot simulate even slightly larger microscopic things like protein molecules, let alone macroscopic things like the human brain. As Robert Laughlin and David Pines so eloquently put it, "predicting protein functionality or the behavior of the human brain from these equations is patently absurd ... We have succeeded in reducing all of ordinary physical behavior to a simple, correct Theory of Everything only to discover that it has revealed exactly nothing about many things of great importance."[4] There is much room for the unknown as we journey from the most fundamental levels of nature to increasingly more complex levels of abstraction: from atoms, to molecules, to cells, to tissues, to systems, to organisms, to societies, and so on. Scientifically speaking, we almost certainly do not know all causal mechanisms that influence the observable behavior of things and people.

Let us look at this in a bit more detail. In 1967, Konrad Zuse postulated that the whole universe could be modeled as a so-called 'cellular automaton.'[5] The idea is that the substrate of nature is analogous to a kind of cosmological computer and the phenomena we observe are the results of computations performed in such a computer. The substrate is postulated to be an immense array of so-called 'cells,' where each cell can be loosely visualized as a microscopic cube of space. The fabric of the universe could then be loosely visualized as an incommensurable array of gazillions of these little cubes, or cells, one next to the other. Each cell is postulated to hold a state at any given moment, which represents the properties of the universe in the particular location of the cell. Computations—that is, the phenomena of nature—are then modeled as changes in the states of the cells. So-called state transition rules govern how the state of each cell changes over time. If Zuse was right, all the fundamental laws of physics discovered at a microscopic level can be modeled algorithmically as particular state transition rules. In fact, a whole new field of physics, called 'digital physics,' has emerged to study this possibility.

Since most of the known physical interactions in nature are local, the next state of any given cell is inferred to depend only on the states of nearby cells. We then say that the evolution of the cell's state depends only on a relatively small 'cell neighborhood' comprising nearby cells. Although this assumption of locality is consistent with experimental observations, it is probably so *by construction*. You see, in order to perform observations under controlled conditions, we must eliminate the potential influence of complex configurations of distant cell states, for in practice the conditions around those cannot be controlled. Consequently, a lot of long-distance effects may be blocked out of the experiments and thus remain undetected.

I do not mean to say that the assumption of locality is entirely unreasonable. After all, the theory of relativity tells us that information can travel no faster than the speed of light. Therefore, a cell cannot exert immediate influence on the state of another cell when they are sufficiently far apart. But it remains a possibility that the size of the cell neighborhood in a correct cellular-automaton model of nature may be much larger than what most scientists today assume. The speed of light is high enough that causal influences could conceivably play out over relatively large scales, if the right configuration of states is present. The neighborhood may thus comprise significantly more cells over significantly longer distances. It may even span more than the three dimensions of space we normally experience. For instance, it may encompass all eleven dimensions of spacetime entailed by M-theory. The neighborhood may also entail a greater variety of possible cell states than we imagine today. For instance, it may entail cell states corresponding to the properties of dark matter and energy. Finally, careful experiments performed in physics laboratories around the world have already shown that non-local, instantaneous interactions at a distance somehow do occur in nature.[6] So the relevant cell neighborhoods could, in theory, comprise the whole universe. All this means that there could be richer, more nuanced and complex state evolution dynamics in nature than those captured in the known laws of physics.

We may still be tempted to think that long-distance causal influences entailed by large cell neighborhoods cannot exist because science has never observed them under controlled conditions. But then again, practical limitations of the experiments that can be carried out may prevent scientists, by construction, from ever triggering those influences in the first place. In practice, one cannot sufficiently control all the conditions and monitor all the parameters that may be relevant to microscopic-level experiments entailing large cell neighborhoods and varied state configurations. One also cannot test all the permutations of experimental conditions and state configurations necessary to trigger unexpected effects. Finally, one does not have the ability to simulate sufficiently complex macroscopic phenomena from microscopic first principles, so we just do not know if our microscopic 'theory of everything' is sufficient to explain the observable world.

There may thus be unknown laws of nature out there directly influencing, right now, the phenomena we observe every day, the things that happen in our lives and perhaps even our own thoughts and behavior. While speculative, this is not at all inconsistent with known science. Notice that I am not talking about the emergence of a certain fact of nature (like consciousness) out of components whose properties are unrelated to it (like neurons or computer chips). Instead, I am only talking about as-of-yet unknown, subtle causal influences that may co-govern the behavior and evolution of nature, including ourselves.

As a matter of fact, some scientists have already acknowledged that certain natural phenomena may not be *even in principle* explainable by microscopic 'theories of everything.' In 1972, Nobel Laureate physicist Philip Warren Anderson discussed this.[7]

His work was later expanded upon by Gu and collaborators.[8] Anderson and Gu listed a number of measurable phenomena for which a microscopic explanation based on subatomic particle behavior does not seem to be sufficient in a fundamental manner.

We seem to live under a collective hallucination that science already has fundamental explanations for everything in our lives, even though it may not have worked out all the details yet. As I hope to have impressed upon you, this is far from the truth, even for most of the trivial everyday phenomena. This assertion is not an attempt to dismiss the success of the scientific endeavor; progress has been enormous and the improvements it has led to in our lives speak for themselves. But it is not scientific to implicitly infer the dominion of existing scientific explanations upon phenomena for which such explanations have not been demonstrated to be sufficient. There is plenty of room left for things we do not know about and may not even imagine today.

# Chapter 7

# The role of intelligence

Philosopher John Searle once proposed a thought experiment that has become notorious and extremely influential in academic circles. It is called the 'Chinese Room' argument[1] and it has been used to highlight an intuition that no computer can ever truly understand anything.

The thought experiment goes like this: a clerk who only speaks English is locked up in a room without windows. Through a small slot in the wall of the room, a Chinese person can pass to him questions written in Chinese. The Chinese person has no idea of whom or what is inside the room. He just passes his questions on paper through the small slot. Inside the room, our English-speaking friend receives the paper filled with Chinese symbols. He has no idea what those symbols mean, but he has a huge manual, written in English, about how to process Chinese symbols so to generate answers in Chinese. His job is this: given the Chinese symbols in the paper received from outside, he must follow the rules in the manual and generate another sequence of Chinese symbols to send back to the outside as a reply to the question originally received. The Chinese person receives the reply from the room and, lo and behold, finds a perfectly reasonable and intelligible answer, *in Chinese*, to the question he had originally asked. He very reasonably assumes then that whatever or whoever is inside the room can understand Chinese.

However, the English-speaking clerk in the room has no idea of what the question was, or the answer for that matter. All he did was to blindly follow rules for manipulating symbols. The rules could go like this: "for such or such groups of Chinese symbols coming in, write such or such groups of Chinese symbols on your reply." The rules should then cover every possible group and combinations of groups of symbols that could occur. Naturally, there would be countless rules of potentially enormous complexity. But we can imagine that the manual is big enough and that the English-speaking clerk inside the room has enough time, enough blank sheets of paper, pencils and filing cabinets to perform the necessary administration.

Now Searle asks the following question: even though from the outside we may believe that the room understands Chinese — since it answers questions in Chinese correctly every time — can a clerk blindly following a set of rules be said to really understand Chinese? Our intuition screams to us: of course not. As Searle so colorfully put it, "such symbol manipulation by itself couldn't be sufficient for understanding Chinese in any literal sense because the man could write 'squoggle squoggle' after 'squiggle squiggle' without understanding anything in Chinese."[2] Analogously, says Searle, computers can never truly be said to understand anything, since all they do is to manipulate symbols according to pre-programmed rules, very much like the English-speaking clerk inside the room. Searle believes that understanding is the result of unique properties — or 'causal powers' — of the brain that no computer simulation can reproduce.

This intuition is incredibly powerful. Yet, the majority of academics today have concluded that the argument actually says nothing about intelligence or about the possibility of computers becoming intelligent. The manual the clerk follows is like a computer program or software. If — as hypothesized in the thought experiment — the software were elaborate and complete enough to generate a correct reply in Chinese every time, then it would indeed be intelligent. After all, unlike consciousness, intelligence is an objective property that can be objectively measured. It is just that the required level of complexity of the software would be so enormous that it would not fit our normal mental picture of a rulebook used by a clerk inside a room. So how can we reconcile the strong intuition we get that the room cannot possibly understand Chinese with the objective fact that it does possess the intelligence required to hold a conversation in Chinese?

To continue further with our exploration, we need a clearer definition of intelligence. Although there are many variations of a definition in the academic world, most of them capture the same fundamental aspects. *An entity is said to be intelligent when it is capable of building internal models of reality by means of which it can interpret past and current events, as well as anticipate future events, with a degree of accuracy and speed.*

In less formal wording, if you have valid internal *explanations* for things that happened and valid internal *predictions* for things that might happen, then you possess a degree of intelligence. You are intelligent if you can, for instance, correctly explain why your bank balance is low this week; and you are even more intelligent if you can explain why the world economy nearly collapsed during the 2007-2009 financial crisis. You are intelligent if you can, for instance, predict that your steak will cook if you put it over a hot grill; and you are even more intelligent if you can predict how global warming will play itself out. The more complete, elaborate and accurate these explanations and predictions are, the more intelligent you will be. The faster you can come up with these predictions and explanations, the more intelligent you will be.

Our brain structures, together with the signals captured by our sensory organs, define an envelope of possible neural symbol manipulations for constructing those explanations and predictions. These neural symbols (which I shall henceforth refer to simply as 'symbols') are the neural *representations* of the things we see, smell, touch, taste and hear. They are also the neural representations of things we have seen, smelled, touched, tasted and heard in the past and whose memories we still hold. For instance, if you look out your window right now and see a tree, the mental image of the tree will correspond to a symbol manipulated inside your brain, which represents the tree 'out there.' The word 'tree' and the sound of its pronunciation also correspond to symbols that may be evoked in your brain, through association, as a consequence of seeing the tree. Even the Chinese character for 'tree' corresponds to one such a symbol in your brain. Similarly, the memory of the smell of a pine tree that you may have cut last Christmas also corresponds to a symbol manipulated in your brain the moment you recall it. For clarity, all of these symbols consist merely of electrochemical signals circulating across your neurons; they may *represent* things like trees, sounds and smells 'out there,' but they are nothing more than measurable, physical neural signals inside your head. The manipulations of such symbols take the form of neural signal processing in the brain, so we can compute valid explanations and predictions about things and events. For instance, you may say: "I could feel the smell of the pine tree so intensely last year because I exposed its internals when I cut it down." Or: "If I prune the tree in the garden later today, I will probably experience a strong woody aroma again." Producing these explanations and predictions through symbol manipulations is the role of intelligence. Once the envelope of possible symbol manipulations is defined as a quantum wave function in the brain, Stapp's theory tells us that consciousness comes into play and chooses one of the possibilities within the envelope. This defines what we actually perceive as objects in consciousness.

Naturally, we often also need to decide on an action. The perception that emerges out of choosing one of the possibilities circumscribed by the symbol manipulations in the brain guides our choice of action. For instance, if a car is speeding towards you and, through symbol manipulations of what you are seeing now and have seen in the past, you predict that you are going to be run over, you will likely choose to get out of the way. The choice of which action to take, still according to Stapp's model, can only be made when consciousness again collapses the wave function that arises in the brain after it has been primed by the prediction that you are going to be run over.

It is important that we differentiate between the mechanical symbol manipulations performed by our neurons and the insight, understanding and other objects in consciousness that we get *along with* such symbol manipulations. Intelligence entails setting up our physical brain structures, in the form of connections between neurons, to construct accurate models of reality. In regular states, consciousness only has access to the symbol manipulations entailed by those models and can only causally affect material reality through those models. Let us discuss this idea of models in a little more detail.

Some video games are familiar examples of computer models. For instance, flight simulators are computer models of real aircraft and of atmospheric conditions. An accurate flight simulator is such that the behavior of the virtual aircraft in the virtual world of the computer simulation corresponds to the behavior of the real aircraft in the real world. This correspondence should be one-to-one; that is, each aspect of the simulated aircraft's behavior should correspond accurately to an aspect of the real aircraft's behavior. In technical jargon, we say that there is an isomorphism—that is, a correspondence of form—between the model used in the simulation and the real thing.

Although the models used in computer games aim simply at providing a marginally accurate simulation of reality for entertainment purposes, accurate models serve a much more practical and important purpose: they enable us to explain and predict reality without having to do the real thing. For instance, an accurate computer model of a tall skyscraper enables engineers to predict its stability and ability to withstand high winds. Engineers can make these predictions before they actually begin building the skyscraper so that, if the building turns out to be unstable, they can make adjustments to the design without having to find out about the errors only after the wrongly designed building collapses. Engineers can also build computer models of structures that have already failed in reality, so as to explain why those failures occurred.

*Models are mirrors of the world.* They comprise internal elements and laws that are isomorphic to elements and laws of the world. The more accurate the isomorphism, the more accurate will the explanations and predictions of the model be. *The symbol manipulations in our brains are themselves models the world. And, as it turns out, all we are self-reflectively aware of are these mirrors of the world inside our heads, not the world itself.*

We are constantly deriving explanations about events we observed and making predictions about future events. Each of these explanations and predictions consists simply of neural signals (symbols) circulating in our brains, but which are expected to represent entities in external reality in an isomorphic manner. This is what intelligence does as a core function of our brains. The more complete and accurate our mental models of reality are, the more intelligent we are. In other words, the more of the elements and laws of nature we can correctly mirror in corresponding neural signals in our brains, the more intelligent we are.

Neuroscientist Henry Markram and his team at the *École Polytechnique Fédérale de Lausanne*, in Switzerland, have been working on computer versions of the structure and dynamics of mammalian brains.[3] Their simulations capture the idiosyncrasies of individual neurons, which have given them unique and detailed insights into how the brain actually functions. With their work, they are addressing the idea discussed above that the brain generates a model of the universe around us, our conscious experiences being defined by such model. In Markram's words, the "theory is that the brain creates, builds, a version of the universe and projects this version of the universe, like a bubble, all around us."[4] Markram uses this idea to interpret, for instance, the way most anesthetics actually work: they do not send us into a deep sleep or block our perceptual receptors, as most people believe. Instead, they work by injecting 'noise' into the brain, disrupting the symbol manipulations entailed by the brain model of the universe. This cripples our ability to consciously register anything coherently, because our consciousness is confined to that model now disrupted. Markram says that "99% of what you see is not what comes in through the eyes; it is what you infer"[5] by means of the model of the universe inside your brain. This is a remarkable assertion that illustrates the extent to which our perceived 'objective reality' is actually determined by the neural models in our heads and how hopelessly confined to these models our regular consciousness is.

Returning to the analogy of robot explorers on Mars, the models responsible for the symbol manipulations in our brains perform a lot of processing on symbols detected by our senses prior to exposure to consciousness. This is analogous to the computations the Martian robotic explorers performed, prior to transmission, on data sent to mission control on Earth. We may be conscious of some of the raw data captured by our senses, but are mostly aware of the resulting explanations and predictions derived from this data by our mental models of reality. In a way, consciousness is trapped inside our mental models, having no direct access to the world, but only to the symbol manipulations in the brain. If the models are not entirely accurate, then inaccurate perceptions arise in consciousness. Since our mental models are never complete—in the sense that they never explain the whole of nature—our consciousness is never aware of the whole of nature. *We are like video gamers who spend their entire lives in a flight simulator, having never even seen a real aircraft, let alone flown one.*

The question now is: How does the brain build these indirect models of reality? How do these models come to incorporate the correct manipulations of symbols? The brain is so enormously complex that it is difficult to answer these questions solely through analysis of a real brain. A complementary approach is an engineering-oriented one: instead of only analyzing the brain, we can also try to *build* something like the brain and see if it works in similar ways. If it does, we will have our answers, since we will know exactly how we built it. Though there are many valid attempts in both academia and industry today to engineer a brain-like electronic system, I will discuss only one, which I consider to be particularly insightful for our purposes: Pentti Haikonen's 'cognitive architecture.'[6]

Haikonen has done advanced artificial intelligence research at Nokia Research Center in Finland. His goal has been to design cognitive computer systems that behave in ways analogous to humans, so they can better interact with humans and do things that, today, only humans can do. His greatest insight has been that *the human brain is but a correlation-finding and association-performing engine.* All the brain does is to find correlations between neural symbols and capture these correlations in symbol associations performed by neurons. In his artificial 'brain,' these associations are performed by artificial associative neurons. All symbols in Haikonen's artificial brain architecture are ultimately linked, perhaps through a long series of associations, to signals from sensory mechanisms. This grounds all symbol associations in discerned things and events of the external world, which gives these associations their semantic value. In this framework, the explanations derived by the brain are just a series of symbol associations linking two past events. The predictions derived by the brain are just extrapolated symbol association chains.

Let us look at some examples to understand this well. Suppose you see someone smile with satisfaction after having taken a bite from a chocolate cake. Your brain instantly conjures up an explanation for that: the person smiled because the cake tastes good. This explanation is the result of symbol associations the brain has been trained to perform over time, while finding naturally occurring correlations between symbols of perception.

Finding and capturing these correlations in Haikonen's associative artificial neurons is analogous to what we call 'learning.' For instance, in the past you may have several times eaten slices of chocolate cake that tasted all very good. This is a naturally occurring correlation between chocolate cake and delicious flavor. From the repetition of this experience, the brain learned over time to associate the perceptual symbol 'chocolate cake' to the perceptual symbol 'delicious flavor.' This association entails the learning that those two symbols tend to occur either together or as a consequence of one another. Your brain may also have learned a correlation, and encoded an association in your neurons, between the symbols 'delicious flavor' and 'smile.' This way, a sequence of two symbol associations leads from 'chocolate cake' to 'smile' via 'delicious flavor.'

Once the symbol associations are in place, they serve as a model to explain observed events, as well as to predict future events. This way, when you see somebody smile after eating chocolate cake, your brain matches those observed symbols to the chain of associations 'chocolate cake' – 'delicious flavor' – 'smile.' You then infer that the person smiled because the chocolate cake tasted good. Similarly, if you are at a restaurant and the waiter places your dessert plate before you containing a slice of chocolate cake, you will predict that you will have the experience of 'delicious flavor' the moment you eat it. This prediction arises because your brain has already encoded—that is, learned from previous observations—an association between 'chocolate cake' and 'delicious flavor.'

It may be difficult to accept that our sophisticated human intelligence can be boiled down to detecting correlations and establishing associations between neural symbols. And this is why the work of Haikonen is so insightful, since he is able to explain myriad brain functions, in great detail, purely based on the idea of symbol associations.

At the moment you were born, your brain likely was a nearly

blank slate (except for whatever instinctive responses may have been genetically encoded in it). It hosted hardly any models. Initially, it received a flood of symbols from the sensory organs that were manipulated in relatively random, chaotic, incoherent ways. Over time, through learning, your brain started realizing that different symbols tended to occur together or in a sequence. The observation of these correlations led to physical modifications in the structure of your brain, slowly turning into mental models of reality. How this can physically take place in the brain has been explained and modeled mathematically, for instance, by Randall O'Reilly and Yuko Munakata.[7] If two symbols have occurred many times in succession in your past, and now the first one of them has just been perceived by your brain, through the associations encoded in it your brain will predict that the second symbol may be about to come. Ultimately, though, *there are only learned associations between symbols, no understanding as such.* It is striking but quite logical, as we will soon see.

Haikonen talks of his cognitive architecture as a conscious machine because, like many others, he seems to assume that a potential for private subjective experience is a property of all material arrangements, a position related to what is usually called 'panpsychism.' For the purposes of this book, it is not important whether this assumption is correct.

Let us now return to our original question, namely: How can we reconcile the strong intuition we get that the 'Chinese Room' cannot possibly understand Chinese, with the objective, measurable fact that it does possess the intelligence required to hold a conversation in Chinese? The logical answer is that *understanding is an object in consciousness that is correlated with symbol associations in the brain, but cannot exist outside consciousness.* The Chinese Room argument makes a separation between the entity that contains the model of reality with corresponding symbol association rules—the manual—and the entity that possesses consciousness—the clerk. This separation renders the jump from symbol associations to true understanding impossible, for the manual itself is not conscious. Even though the conscious clerk is performing the symbol associations himself, one at a time, following the rules in the manual, he does not have an internalized model in his own brain that could lead to understanding.

The strong intuition that we get from the Chinese Room argument has nothing to do with intelligence, but with consciousness. Searle is appealing to the sense of insight and understanding we have as humans. Insight and understanding are correlates in consciousness of certain intelligent processes taking place in the physical brain. The latter consist simply of symbol associations performed according to the rules imposed by the structure and electrochemistry of the neural networks in the brain, akin to the clerk following the rules in a manual. However, in the Chinese Room, the model is in the manual whereas consciousness is in the clerk, so the symbol associations can never translate into a conscious insight of understanding. The Chinese Room argument shows that, when separating the entity with assumed consciousness (the clerk) from the unconscious intelligent model (the manual), true understanding of the model cannot occur. This clearly highlights our strong intuition that understanding only exists in consciousness, not in intelligence. Symbol associations reflect intelligence, but not understanding.

On the other hand, when the symbol associations occur in the physical brain, they lead to the conscious *feeling* of insight and understanding because, as we discussed earlier, the brain is the transceiver of consciousness. This is what we have as humans that an extremely intelligent but unconscious computer would not have. As we argued earlier, this is not just a matter of material complexity, but of a fundamental fact of nature (consciousness) for which we have an explanatory gap in science today.

If the brain is a transceiver for the interaction between consciousness and the material aspects of reality, then the symbol associations taking place in the physical brain are responsible for constructing the messages that are transmitted to consciousness. Searle's Chinese Room argument appeals to our intuition that understanding, as an object in consciousness, cannot happen if that transmission does not take place. In the Chinese Room, the transmission never happens because intelligence and consciousness are separated from each other as properties of different entities.

Critics of Searle have argued against the validity of the Chinese Room argument by pointing out that the clerk is just a part of a system comprising the clerk himself and the manual. The critics argue that it is the whole system that understands Chinese, not the clerk alone. Searle counters this argument in a straightforward way: imagine that the clerk has now memorized the entire manual, with all its symbol manipulation rules. This way, you can now forget about the manual and only consider the clerk. He has the entire model in his brain. But the clerk still just follows memorized rules. Does the clerk now truly understand Chinese?

Think about it for a moment. The clerk memorized the manual, but he is still just blindly following rules for associating symbols whose meaning he ignores. So the clerk still does not understand Chinese at all. This seems pretty self-evident and Searle's original argument ends here.

But if you have been reading attentively, you will have noticed that I just put myself in an apparently difficult position here. My original argument was that intelligence and consciousness were separated from each other as properties of different entities, so there could be no understanding. However, the symbol association rules that originally were in the manual now are in the brain of the entity that has consciousness (the clerk). There is no longer any separation between rules and consciousness. So how come is there still no understanding? The onus is on me to explain this without contradicting my earlier argument. And here is the explanation: there is still no understanding because a crucial element of a true model of reality is still missing from the clerk's head. It is subtle, but glaringly obvious once you see it. Bear with me.

Let us go back to Haikonen's idea of the brain as a correlation-finding and association-performing engine of neural symbols. His key insight is that the brain can perform many cognitive functions simply by associating symbols of different modalities that ultimately signify the same thing. For instance, the mental image of a tree—with its trunk, branches and leaves—corresponds to a neural symbol that *directly* represents an external entity; a mirror-image in our heads of an entity in the outside world. On the other hand, the mental image of the English *word* 'tree,' with its four letters, corresponds to a neural symbol of a clearly different modality, but which ultimately signifies the same thing *in*directly: the mental image of the *word* 'tree' evokes the mental image of a tree, which, *in turn*, represents a real tree 'out there.' The word 'tree' would be meaningless if not for its evocation of mental images of trees. Similarly, the *sound* we get when we pronounce the English word 'tree' corresponds to a neural symbol of yet another modality, which indirectly represents the same entity of the outside world. For emphasis: the mental image of the tree corresponds to a neural symbol that *directly* mirrors external reality in the brain, whereas the symbols associated with the *word* 'tree' (written or spoken) are neural 'labels' that refer *in*directly to external reality. The brain learns the correlations between these direct and indirect symbols: sound 'tree' – written word 'tree' – mental image of a tree. This way, when we hear the sound 'tree' or see the written word 'tree,' the image of a real tree pops in our minds through learned association. This is how we understand language. *Without this grounding of all indirect language-related symbols in perceptual symbols corresponding directly to entities of external reality, one could not possibly understand language.* Without it, any language would feel to you as a foreign language that you never learned.

When we imagine the clerk memorizing the entire manual of Chinese symbol manipulations, we are leaving out all the associations between the indirect language symbols (representing Chinese characters) and the direct perceptual symbols (corresponding to mental images, sounds, flavors, aromas, feelings, etc.) that ground them in entities of external reality. In fact, it is only the Chinese person outside the room that, upon receiving the written answer from the room, can perform the necessary associations between Chinese characters and entities of external reality. Therefore, even if the clerk memorized the entire manual he would still not have the complete model of reality, with its corresponding symbol associations, in his head. We can then conclude that my original argument still holds: while the clerk now has internalized parts of the model of reality (the manual), he still does not have a crucial part of the model in his brain (the grounding of language symbols in external entities of reality). This way, the transmission to consciousness is not complete in a very fundamental way and there can be no understanding.

Now let us extend the thought experiment a bit ourselves. If the clerk, having internalized the entire manual, were also to learn the associations between each Chinese character and the entity of external reality it refers to, then I guess we would be safe in saying that he would indeed understand Chinese. In fact, this would be the very definition of learning a new language: the manual would give him the grammatical and syntactical rules of the Chinese language, while the grounding of the Chinese characters in entities of external reality would give him the semantics. But notice this: the key reason why we feel comfortable with this conclusion is that *we assume the clerk to be a conscious entity like ourselves*, thereby fulfilling the most important intuitive requirement for the ability to understand. So the room now understands Chinese because the clerk—a conscious human—understands Chinese himself.

Now imagine that there is no human clerk in the Chinese Room, but only a supercomputer programmed with all the Chinese symbol manipulation rules originally in the clerk's manual and equipped with Internet access. This way, the supercomputer would have sensory inputs in the form of images downloaded from the Internet. Assume too that we would further program the supercomputer with all symbol association rules necessary for linking each Chinese character to corresponding digital image files downloaded from the Internet. For instance, a digital photograph of a tree would be linked to the Chinese character for 'tree.' Would the supercomputer now truly understand Chinese? Could mere software links between digital symbols and digital images be the crucial difference that confers understanding, even though there is no subjective experience of these symbols and images?

I know that, in appealing to your intuition with the questions above, I am doing more hand waving than logical argumentation. However, it is my contention that the very notion of *understanding* resides eminently in conscious experience. My use of the modified Chinese Room argument above aims at highlighting precisely this. If such contention is correct, there is no alternative but to argue about the notion of understanding in the subjective framework where the notion itself exists. I thus submit that the supercomputer would still have no true understanding, despite the software links between Chinese characters and digital images, as long as the supercomputer were not conscious.

When one considers the inner workings of the brain, one is looking at the processes of intelligence. In the absence of consciousness, intelligence consists purely of mechanical symbol associations, grounded in external reality or not, like what the clerk in the Chinese room does with the help of his gigantic manual. Symbol associations are just the neural *correlates* of objects in consciousness, not self-reflective experiences in and of themselves. Searle's Chinese Room argument, with the extensions we discussed above, helps us gain a strong intuition about the difference between these two things: whenever we separate crucial symbol associations from an assumed conscious entity, our intuition tells us that *understanding* of these symbol associations is no longer possible.

As a final note, I want to make sure I do not misrepresent Searle's points of view here. Searle does not believe that consciousness—or 'intentionality,' which is the technical term he actually uses—is the fundamental substrate or 'substance' of reality. He does not believe the brain to be a transceiver of immaterial consciousness. In fact, he believes that consciousness is a property of the structure and electrochemistry of the brain, therefore being generated by the brain itself. He does not believe that electronic computers can manifest consciousness because computers today do not *replicate*, but merely *simulate*, this structure and electrochemistry. According to Searle, it is as-of-yet unknown "causal powers" of the structure and electrochemistry of the brain that allow consciousness—and therefore understanding—to exist. Although Searle does not identify what these causal powers are, here I associate them with whatever features of the brain allow for the interaction of immaterial consciousness with the material world. In other words, for me the equivalent of Searle's "causal powers of intentionality" are the specific structures and electrochemical properties of the brain that allow it to work as a consciousness transceiver, whatever those specific structures and electrochemical properties may be. According to Stapp's theory, it is the quantum mechanical nature of the movement of calcium ions in nerve terminals that make up such "causal powers of intentionality."

Whatever the origin or cause of consciousness, Searle's arguments clearly highlight *the importance of there being consciousness for the ability of an entity to have true understanding.* This is the point where Searle's arguments fit into the thought-line of this book.

Let us go back to our inference that the brain is a transceiver of consciousness in material reality. Consciousness only has access to the symbol associations taking place inside the brain, not to the external world. However, since the brain builds indirect neural models of external reality, which operate through those symbol associations, consciousness can have *in*direct access to the outside world. The structure and electrochemistry of the brain frame the perception of whatever the external reality might be, before presenting it to consciousness. Therefore, *disturbances or damage to the way the brain physically operates immediately affect and modulate our conscious perception of the world,* even though consciousness, as inferred, does not arise from the brain itself. This explains the correlations between brain states and subjective experience.

## Chapter 8

# The beginnings of a theory of purpose

We now have to revisit a question we left open in an earlier chapter: why would nature impose on itself limitations analogous to the ones faced by interplanetary explorers operating robotic vehicles from a distance? If consciousness is the primary ground of meaning, why would nature choose to trap consciousness within the narrow confines of brains? It does not seem to make sense. Yet, we arrived at this crossroads by following a coherent line of thought. Therefore, the question is certainly deserving of careful consideration.

One could argue that consciousness is simply *on its way* to expansion and enrichment. The path to expansion may entail that, in the current stage of universal evolution, consciousness *happens* to be limited to the capabilities of current brain structures and associated models of reality. However, the brain itself can be expected to continue to evolve and improve over generations, thereby easing the limitations imposed on consciousness. The models of reality that brains are capable of building can become increasingly more comprehensive, sophisticated and accurate, thereby giving consciousness access to more and more elements and laws of nature, as mirrored in these neural models. In this context, although the conscious experience of nature remains always indirect, operating through nature's reflection on mental models, the current limitations of consciousness are seen simply as a natural stage in its path to enrichment. It can be inferred that, at some point in the universe's evolution, such limitations will gradually erode through material betterment and consciousness will expand to yet unknown depth and scope.

At first sight, the hypothesis above may sound entirely consistent with what we have articulated so far. It seems to correspond perfectly to the natural process of enrichment that we have inferred earlier to take place in nature and to give it its meaning. However, more careful analysis shows us that such is not the case. In fact, the hypothesis is based on the subtle assumption that consciousness is fundamentally *circumscribed by* material reality, its depth and scope being a consequence of the evolution of material structures (for instance, brains). In other words, it is assumed that the reach of consciousness fundamentally depends on structures of material reality. Only then does it make sense to infer that consciousness is enriched *as* such structures of material reality themselves evolve.

But earlier we have argued the exact opposite of this: that consciousness has primacy over material reality. We have also argued that it is material reality that is a consequence of consciousness, not the other way around. To base this position, we have used two arguments: first, the fact that we do not have direct access to a reality outside consciousness and that all we believe to exist are, in fact, objects in our own consciousness; and second, the fact that Wigner's interpretation of quantum mechanics places observation in consciousness as a precondition for physical existence. Therefore, the hypothesis that consciousness expands merely as a consequence of brain evolution is not logically consistent with our articulation so far.

So we are still left with our original question: If consciousness is the primary ground of meaning, as inferred in previous chapters, why would nature choose to trap consciousness within the narrow confines of physical brains? We have seen above that whatever the answer to this question may be, it cannot entail that the enrichment of consciousness is circumscribed or paced by the evolution of structures in material reality. What other hypotheses are we left with?

The only avenue left is that the very imposition of limitations on consciousness through material structures is the vehicle for its expansion. Now, this sounds totally illogical at first. It sounds like saying that you can lose weight by eating more, or something similarly contradictory. But there is a surprising way in which this makes sense. In fact, there is a way in which this may explain your existence right now, including the fact that you are reading this book. To gain insight into it, however, we need to briefly touch upon what science calls 'information theory.'

Engineer and mathematician Claude Shannon, the founder of information theory, published a highly influential scientific paper in 1948, the concepts of which underlie all electronic communications today.[1] Every phone call you make, every page you download from the Internet, every show you watch on television has been made possible by the theoretical framework outlined by Shannon. His key insight in the paper has been to find a way to quantify what we call 'information.'

Shannon succeed in quantifying information by using the framework of a system where a transmitter selects one among a set of possible messages and sends it to a receiver. You could think of the receiver and transmitter respectively as you and a friend of yours talking on the phone. Suppose you called your friend to ask how he is doing. There is an enormous number of messages he could then select to transmit to you in reply. Namely, he could say that he is doing 'well,' or 'terribly,' or 'strange,' or even that he is 'unsure.' According to Shannon, the more possible messages your friend can pick from as an answer to transmit to you, the more information there will be in that one single answer. To understand Shannon's insight, imagine that you call your friend merely to know if he is at home. There are then only two possible messages that can be transmitted: yes (for instance, if he picks up the phone himself) or no (for instance, if nobody picks up the phone). There is then less information in the message, whether it is 'yes' or 'no,' since the number of possible messages is restricted to only two. As Shannon put it, "the number of [possible] messages … can be regarded as a measure of the information produced when one message is chosen."[2]

This is very logical. If your friend answers 'well' to the question of how he is doing, this excludes a whole lot of other possibilities. Therefore, he is in fact telling you a lot in this one single answer. By saying that he is doing well he is also saying that he knows how he is doing (so he is not unsure), that he is not doing terribly, or just OK, etc. This single answer comprises information about many other possibilities regarding how he is doing. On the other hand, if nobody picks up the phone when you call him to check if he is at home, the implied message excludes only one other possibility—namely, that he is at home—so it does not convey much information at all.

The information content of a message received is a measure of how many other possible states of the transmitter can be discerned from it. The higher the number of possible transmitter states, the more information there is in any message received from it. As such, the smallest amount of information is that contained in a 'bit': a message that communicates one of only two possible states, such as 'yes' or 'no,' 'zero' or 'one.' Consequently, information only exists when at least two states are possible: one corresponding to the *foreground* (that is, the message received, such as 'one,' which then becomes the state of the receiver) and the other corresponding to the *background* (that is, the other possible state of the transmitter, such as 'zero,' which provides a contrast that gives meaning to the foreground).

Now, the important point is this: *the universal process of consciousness enrichment discussed in Chapters 3 and 4 depends on some form of information inflow,* so that something can be learned. After all, what new conscious insight can be gained when there are no 'news' coming in to trigger it? It is the perception of novelty associated with information inflow that motivates consciousness to 'move,' so to realize its intrinsic potentials. Without the foreground/background contrast entailed by the distinction between its own state and other possible states of a hypothetical external transmitter, consciousness would take its foreground state for granted and never become explicitly aware of it. There would be nothing to learn. Without an inflow of perceived novelty to contrast with its own state, there would be no disturbance or stimulus to kick consciousness out of its *status quo*, nothing to compare itself to. On the other hand, the more information comes in from the hypothetical transmitter, the more heightened the sense of curiosity associated with it and the higher the motivation of consciousness to somehow make sense of, and accommodate, this incoming information in relation to itself. Information inflow thus triggers inquiry, a necessary first step towards *self*-inquiry.

Importantly, as we learned from Shannon, the higher the number of possible background states of the hypothetical external transmitter, the more information inflow and learning can there be and the greater the associated novelty value. Keep this idea in mind for now. We will return to it shortly after we add, below, one more necessary ingredient to the storyline.

Earlier, we could not find a logical reason for why the universe would be such that consciousness is trapped within the narrow confines of brains. Such entrapment seems utterly unnatural and inconsistent with what we surmise about the nature of consciousness. Having found ourselves facing this dilemma, the only alternative left is *to hypothesize that such an entrapment somehow was not the original state of nature.* Perhaps nature was, originally, such that consciousness was boundless. A boundless consciousness seamlessly encompassing the obfuscated mind would, in fact, be consistent with Wigner's interpretation of quantum mechanics, as well as with the philosophical view that consciousness precedes material reality ontologically.

There is a profound implication to this hypothesis. *If consciousness was boundless, then consciousness was necessarily one.* A boundless consciousness would *directly* experience all there is in the universe, thereby eliminating the possibility of separate, individualized streams of experience. Indeed, if you and I were concurrently conscious of each other's thoughts—that is, neural symbol associations—there would be no difference between objects in my consciousness and those in yours. Our consciousnesses would be effectively one and the same.

This notion of one consciousness permeating the entire universe, directly experiencing all there is in it, seems strikingly powerful. However, there would have been no background/ foreground contrast from the point of view of such a unified consciousness. The reason is subtle but crucial to our argument: *conscious entities identify themselves with whatever they experience directly.* In the case of human beings, we identify ourselves with the neural models in our heads, which give us our sense of identity (indeed, you would still have the same sense of identity if you lost a limb, so you do not really identify yourself with the rest of your body). Boundless consciousness would also naturally identify itself with whatever it would *directly* experience, *which would be all there is.* This way, there would be nothing that it would *not* identify itself with; there would be nothing that it would *not* be; there would be no foreground receiver state discernible from other possible background transmitter states. For this reason, *information inflow is impossible in a hypothetical state of unified, all-encompassing consciousness.*

Moreover, without a separate background reference on the basis of which it could define itself as an entity, an all-encompassing consciousness could not become explicitly aware of its own existence. This, too, would preclude the unfolding of the universal process of consciousness enrichment: Without some form of self-awareness, how could the all-encompassing consciousness be driven towards new insights about itself so to realize its intrinsic potentials?

And there is a yet deeper, more complete state of self-awareness: the awareness not only of your self, but of your own awareness. For instance, I am convinced that my cat is conscious.

I am also convinced that my cat has some conception of itself as an individual entity distinct from me and other cats, for it seems to experience the needs and wishes associated with being such an entity: it seeks food when it feels hunger; it feels the drive to defend its individual territory from other cats; it seeks protection and reassurance when afraid of getting hurt; etc. But I am not at all convinced that my cat is self-aware *in the sense of being aware of its own awareness*, the way you and I are. It experiences needs and wishes but it does not consciously know *that* it experiences needs and wishes.

This deeper state of self-awareness, often called *self-reflection* or *conscious metacognition*, is a key enabler of discovery and understanding because it allows us to analyze and evaluate *our own thought processes*. Through it, we can question and criticize our own logic and conclusions, thereby refining our mental processes. We can frame our analysis itself as an object of meta-analysis, which in turn can be framed as an object of meta-meta-analysis, and so on. Thus, from now on, let us understand self-awareness in this deeper sense. You are self-aware because you are aware that you are aware … that you are aware of your own awareness. This is an infinite recursion of self-awareness that plays out in our minds in finite time, like Zeno's paradox of Achilles and the tortoise.[3] And all of it is only possible because we conceive of ourselves as individuals (the foreground) separate from others and from our environment (the background).

You may have had the experience, during difficult times in life, of observing yourself in despair. It is like there are two of you: a 'subject you' going through the emotion of despair and a 'witness you' observing the 'subject you.' The 'witness you' may even say to 'himself' with surprising calm and composure: "look how sad and desperate I am right now, how the world seems to be falling over my head." This reflects 'his' awareness that the 'subject you' has awareness. It allows the 'witness you' to analyze the experiences and emotions of the 'subject you' and try to establish causal relationships. It allows 'him' to learn about the 'subject you;' that is, to learn about himself. Yet 'he' does all that as if looking from above, watching the world fall under his feet. We are only able to have this dissociated experience because we very clearly conceive of ourselves as entities separate from the world. It is this separateness of identity that creates the 'subject you' going through the emotions of despair, so the 'witness you' can observe and learn about it in a self-aware manner. Separateness from a contextual background is essential to self-awareness.

It is ironic how the very state of all-encompassing consciousness thus seems to preclude self-awareness. Indeed, our ability to be self-reflectively aware of nature seems to be a consequence of the very fact that our consciousness is trapped inside our brain. It is this entrapment that allows us to perceive ourselves as individualized foreground beings separate from the background of other entities in the universe, so we can learn about these other entities and about ourselves.

Wait a moment. Here is our answer, staring us in the face.

If the original state of nature entailed boundless unified consciousness, then—contradictorily as it may sound—such state would have prevented consciousness from becoming aware of itself and its properties in a self-reflective manner. Nonetheless, the very existence of consciousness would have entailed the potential for self-awareness. It is this originally *unrealized potential* that would have left room for a *process of universal enrichment*. If this was so, we can then reasonably postulate the existence of an intrinsic universal tendency for the realization of that potential, since this seems to be the only conceivable reason for the dynamic existence we are all witnesses and parts of.

This universal tendency towards the enrichment of consciousness would have led to an unfolding of natural events such that the unified consciousness would have become 'fragmented,' in a way. The 'fragmentation' would have enabled the creation of a foreground/background dynamics in the universe. Different 'fragments' of the originally unified consciousness would have become individualized. Each individualized consciousness would then have become capable of identifying itself as a foreground in contrast to a background of other natural entities, including other individualized consciousnesses. Only then could each 'fragment' stand outside its own nature, so to contemplate and study this nature with the curiosity and self-reflection capacity of an explorer. Only by becoming individuals seemingly separate from the world could these explorers apprehend the world anew, at a metacognitive level, intrigued by the novelty value of the information inflow assaulting their senses. From the point of view of each individualized consciousness, the rest of nature would have turned into an external 'transmitter' with countless possible states, each message received from this 'transmitter' thus entailing unfathomable information and associated insights. This seeming separation between observer and observed, 'receiver' and 'transmitter,' meant that the underlying nature of reality could no longer take itself for granted. It kicked consciousness out of its static state and unleashed a highly dynamic process of enrichment through self-exploration by proxy.

The 'fragmentation' of unified consciousness allowed an individualized 'fragment' of consciousness to interact with other individualized 'fragments,' accumulating understanding about their behavior, motivations, aspirations, feelings, etc. This, ultimately, means an accumulation of understanding about the unified Self. By means of 'fragmentation,' unified consciousness could learn about itself through the observation of 'fragments' of itself by other 'fragments' of itself; the creation of subject and object from a unit, for the purpose of self-understanding.

This must have been the history of us: from a single boundless consciousness to the individualized and limited conscious beings we now are. And, counter-intuitive as it may be, from a logical perspective this was not a step backward, but one forward in the enrichment of consciousness.

Following this line of thought to its natural conclusion, we can infer that material reality is the means by which consciousness becomes individualized. The material world creates an 'information playing field,' if you will, for the foreground/background dynamics necessary to the ultimate goal of understanding and self-awareness. When 'fragments' of an originally unified consciousness interact with the universe through the confines of material brains, their awareness becomes restricted to the indirect neural models of reality each brain hosts in its structure. Similarly, the memory records associated with each brain confer upon each 'fragment' of consciousness the illusion of having a separate identity.

Notice that a process of enrichment logically could never fundamentally eliminate an originally realized potential of consciousness. This would contradict our entire articulation thus far. A consciousness that once was as broad as to be all-encompassing could not fundamentally lose some of its own reach and scope. Therefore, at the most fundamental level of nature, *consciousness must still be all-encompassing and boundless.*

Consequently, the process of consciousness 'fragmentation' inferred above must rather have entailed the creation of a self-imposed *illusion* of fragmentation. Our intelligence, with the indirect models of reality it encompasses, is the mechanism for the creation of such an illusion. In this context, any *direct* awareness of the world would allow our consciousness to break out of the confines of the brain, return to its intrinsic boundless state and defeat the purpose of individualization. By confining consciousness to the indirect models of reality of our intelligence, nature enables a natural process of evolution towards understanding and self-awareness.

We can visualize this hypothesis in the following way: unified consciousness is like a field. This field, all-encompassing as it is, permeates all of nature. The presence of certain material structures—such as brains—in the physical world indicates that, at the corresponding locations, the field has taken on a localized configuration conducive to the rise of self-reflection. This configuration allows the field to manifest itself in physical form and interact with the physical world through intelligent mental models.

In a way, this may be analogous to the electromagnetic field we call radio waves. Radio waves are everywhere, whether you have a suitable receiver or not. If you are driving your car, whenever you turn on your car radio—which is a suitable material structure for the manifestation of the field—it plays music. Nonetheless, you may drive around town all day with your radio off and never realize that there are radio waves permeating the entire space you are driving through. Still, the fact that your radio is off does not change anything about the existence of the electromagnetic field permeating space. Similarly, a field of consciousness may be everywhere, but interact with the material world only when suitable material structures—brains—are present and functioning.

Continuing on with our analogy, the electromagnetic field of the radio waves is unified and all-encompassing in a certain sense. It is emitted from a transmitter antenna as a single signal broadcast in all directions. When the information in the radio wave is tapped and translated into sound waves by an individual radio receiver, the all-encompassing electromagnetic field becomes *individualized* as it is embodied in this specific radio receiver. The driver can then change radio stations, adjust the volume, equalization and otherwise interact with the broadcast signal in myriad unique, individual manners. In fact, different drivers can set up their car radios so as to receive different stations or equalize the sound in totally different ways. Each car radio may end up sounding very different from the others. However, none of those individual interactions can change the fundamentally unified nature of the radio signal that is being broadcast.

If consciousness is, fundamentally, an all-encompassing and unified field permeating the whole universe like a radio broadcast signal, physical brains may be the transceivers through which this field becomes individualized. The neural structures of our brains, which host indirect models of reality, are the means by which the illusion of separateness is created. Awareness becomes trapped in the dynamics of our neurons, preventing an easy return to a state of direct, boundless experience. The consistent history reflected in the memories experienced by each transceiver creates the illusion of a separate identity. Through such crucial illusion, information inflow becomes possible and a process of progressive build-up of understanding and self-awareness can take place.

As a matter of fact, the fascinating experiences of Dr. Jill Bolte Taylor are very telling in this regard. Dr. Taylor is a scientist, a neural anatomist who has had the unique opportunity to observe herself from within while having a massive brain stroke. As the stroke progressively incapacitated the left side of her brain, Dr. Taylor felt her consciousness expand way beyond her physical body. In her words: "I felt enormous and expansive, like a genie just liberated from her bottle. And my spirit soared free like a great whale, gliding through a sea of silent euphoria. ... I remember thinking there is no way I would ever be able to squeeze the enormousness of myself back inside this tiny little body."[4]

It is striking how a specific brain *malfunction* seems to have allowed Dr. Taylor's individualized consciousness to partially and temporarily jump back to its boundless and unified state. Nonetheless, Dr. Taylor's description is exactly what one would have logically expected if the hypothesis we are now discussing—that of the brain as a mechanism for creating an illusion of consciousness individualization—is correct. If the mechanism gets damaged in *just the right way*, it is logical to infer that the illusion may lift partially and temporarily.

The questions that immediately arise are then: First, are the experiences of Dr. Taylor an isolated event or are there statistically significant instances of analogous cases? And second, where exactly in the brain does the kind of damage that leads to experiences of self-transcendence, such as those undergone by Dr. Taylor, take place? As fortune would have it, science has preliminary answers to both questions. For example, in a paper published in the respected neuroscience journal *Neuron*,[5] an Italian team of neuroscientists studied 88 patients who had undergone brain surgery for the removal of tumors. In many of these patients, surgery had caused localized collateral damage to specific regions of the cerebral cortex. The team of scientist assessed, both before and after surgery, each patient's predisposition to spiritual feelings. Particularly, they assessed each patient's ability to transcend the personal self and feel somehow connected to the universe as a whole. By comparing these psychological assessments done respectively before and after damage had been done to the brain, the team were able to pinpoint the exact regions of the brain that, once damaged, caused an increased feeling of self-transcendence. The study showed that, in a statistically significant number of cases, damage to small, highly localized regions of the left inferior parietal lobe and the right angular gyrus was associated with a significant increase in feelings of self-transcendence shortly after surgery, indicating a direct causal link.

Here, I am interpreting the results obtained by the Italian neuroscientists in the context of the transceiver model of brain-consciousness interaction discussed earlier. More than this, in my view their results are consistent with, and supportive of, such transceiver model. Naturally, the same results can also be interpreted in a different way. Namely, it can be argued that they indicate that consciousness is generated *by* the brain, so that damage to the brain qualitatively modulates subjective experience. But think about this for a moment: Assuming that subjective experience is indeed generated by, and confined to, the physical brain, having no reality outside it, how could damage to the brain lead to the experience of transcending the very system that generates it? On the other hand, if consciousness inherently extends beyond the material constraints of the brain, as posited in this book, it is indeed very natural and logical that specific damage to the brain could result in feelings of self-transcendence. The brain possibly works as a kind of filter of consciousness, evolved to increase survival fitness through enabling focused attention to stimuli directly relevant to survival. This idea is not new and has been popularized in the 1950s by Aldous Huxley, in his quote of philosopher C. D. Broad: "The suggestion is that the function of the brain and nervous system and sense organs is in the main *eliminative* and not productive. Each person is at each moment capable of ... perceiving everything that is happening everywhere in the universe. The function of the brain and nervous system is to protect us from being overwhelmed ... by shutting out most of what we should otherwise perceive or remember at any moment, and leaving only that very small and special selection which is likely to be practically useful."[6] Specific brain damage could compromise the effectiveness of this filter, allowing the underlying self-transcendent experiences—ever present in potential—to be imprinted onto physical memory. A brain-consciousness interaction mechanism like Stapp's model could then provide a means for such imprinting through wave function collapse.

Boundless consciousness could only conceive, understand and become aware of itself if it could experience *not being* itself as such. It could only conceive, understand and become aware of its own all-encompassing nature if it could experience *limitation*. It could only conceive, understand and become aware of its own unified nature if it could experience *fragmentation*. Ironically, it seems that only through an illusory confinement of consciousness can nature realize its potential for self-understanding and self-awareness in a process of consciousness enrichment. The material world can be inferred to be an instrument of this process.

But we are not done yet. In fact, something of enormous significance seems to be lost when consciousness is individualized, even if such individualization is purely illusory: *we lose the experience of direct acquaintance with the rest of nature.* To return to a handy analogy, it would probably be effective for the smart folks at NASA's mission control to ultimately go to Mars themselves, to experience Mars *directly*, after having accumulated all relevant *information* about it through their robotic transceivers.

# Chapter 9

# Recapping our journey thus far

Let us briefly recap our articulation before taking the next logical step. We started our journey by making two fundamental assumptions: the first, that there is indeed an ultimate purpose for life and existence in general; and the second, that this ultimate purpose can be at least partially understood by the human intellect. We inferred that existence can only have meaning if the universe, in its present form, is somehow not yet complete, in the sense that some of its potentials have not yet been realized. This way, the meaning of existence is to realize those potentials, thereby enriching the universe. We also discussed how the posited incompleteness of the universe is entirely consistent with—and perhaps even necessary to—the notion of perfection.

We went on to posit that consciousness is the primary fact of nature, upon which existence depends. We justified this based on the scientific understanding of human perception and its philosophical implications, as well as on Wigner's interpretation of quantum mechanics. The latter takes consciousness to be the causal agency of material reality. We then inferred that, as the primary ground of existence, it must be the potentials of consciousness itself that must be realized so the universe can become complete. The meaning of existence, then, is a universal process of consciousness enrichment.

The empirical fact that brain states are highly correlated with subjective experience allowed us to infer that the brain is a transceiver of immaterial consciousness in material reality. We referred to the quantum mind theory of Henry Stapp as a possible physical mechanism for the realization of this transceiver. With extensions of the Chinese Room thought experiment, we discussed the relationship between consciousness and intelligence. We inferred that intellectual prowess is just an indirect means, or a vehicle, to bring information about relationships and correlations to awareness. This way, our intelligence creates neural models of the world through symbol associations, and it is only through these models that we become aware of the world. In fact, in regular states of consciousness all we are aware of are these models—nothing else. Our consciousness is thus individualized, but limited to the ability of the material brain to capture and mirror external reality. However, the insight of understanding—the "Aha!" of comprehension—resides in consciousness, not in the brain.

A problem then became inescapable: Why would nature be such that consciousness, the primary ground of existence, is trapped in the confines of material brains? Our analysis indicated that this would be a logical contradiction, so we postulated that the original state of consciousness must have been one of boundlessness. Consciousness, as such, would have experienced all of existence directly. We also inferred that such boundless state logically requires consciousness to have been unified.

Based on the concept of information, we inferred that an illusion of fragmentation and individualization of consciousness was necessary, at some point in the cosmological past, for an enrichment of consciousness through understanding and self-awareness. Still, to remain consistent with the idea that the universe is enriching itself—as opposed to losing some of its own potentials—we concluded that, at its most fundamental level, consciousness must still be boundless and unified, like a field.

# Chapter 10

# A return to boundless consciousness

The ultimate purpose of existence is an enrichment of consciousness with understanding and self-awareness, both of which may be just different names for the same idea. As we have seen, this enrichment takes place necessarily through an initial 'fragmentation' and confinement of consciousness to physical transceivers. Only through this illusory fragmentation and confinement are understanding and self-awareness possible.

As understanding and self-awareness grow, consciousness expands. We see more, in a figurative sense. We understand more of the cause and effect relationships in the universe. We gather more insight about its properties and the way it works. Once all potentials are ultimately realized, the illusion of individualization will have served its purpose. At that moment — it is logical to infer — the illusion of fragmentation, individuality and limits will be lifted. The universe will be complete in its comprehension and awareness of itself. Consciousness will return to its intrinsic, boundless state of unity, but now enriched with complete understanding and recursive self-awareness.

*The meaning of life is a gradual return to a unified, boundless state of consciousness enriched by the understanding and self-awareness accumulated during material experience through the transceivers of consciousness.*

We have seen that consciousness, under the illusion of confinement, is limited to the amount and quality of information about the universe that can be mirrored in our mental models. So the illusion of confinement is necessary: it allows the gathering of information. On the other hand — and this is a crucial point — *the reality of boundlessness allows for each individual experience originating from exposure to that information to seamlessly percolate through the whole of universal consciousness.* This is the mechanism by which we, as individuals, can contribute to the ultimate goal of the whole. Therefore, the illusion of fragmentation *and* the reality of boundless unity must *both* be an inherent part of *each moment* of our lives.

The considerations above indicate that, in principle, it should be possible for us to be aware of our boundless nature while physically alive. Indeed, there is nothing in the logic we have followed thus far to suggest that a temporary or partial return to a state of boundlessness is impossible for an individualized consciousness. A *permanent* loss of that individualization by all conscious entities *prior* to an accumulation of sufficient insight from information would violate our articulation, but not a temporary or partial one.

What then is this boundless state of consciousness that, as inferred above, humans must be able to experience in life? Is there any evidence that this has ever been achieved by anyone? Religious and spiritual literature abounds with testimonials of people who claim to have done so as a result of meditation, prayer, psychedelic substances or even spontaneously. In fact, many religious books have been written on it, so I will seek different perspectives here: I will try psychiatric and psychological perspectives.

In the first year of the 20th century, psychiatrist Dr. Richard Maurice Bucke first published an evolutionary theory of consciousness.[1] According to Dr. Bucke, individualized consciousness evolves through four stages: "perceptual mind," "receptual mind," "conceptual mind," and "intuitional mind." In the stage of perceptual mind, there is actually no individualized consciousness. A perceptual mind, in Dr. Bucke's terminology, is akin to what we today would regard as a computer equipped with a few sensory devices like cameras and microphones. Perceptual symbols from the cameras and microphones are processed by the computer, but this processing is supposedly not accompanied by private inner experience. In the second stage, or receptual mind, perceptual symbols are associated together to form higher-order compound symbols Dr. Bucke calls "recepts." Going back to Haikonen's cognitive architecture, recepts would be analogous to internal compound symbols derived from associations between different percepts, the associations being performed by associative neurons. The manipulation of recepts in the brain is postulated to be accompanied by simple states of individualized consciousness, akin to animal consciousness. In the third stage, or conceptual mind, Dr. Bucke brings in language. Language—as we discussed when talking about the Chinese Room argument— is a collection of indirect symbols, or labels, that refer to recepts and percepts. In much of human reasoning, the labels of language actually replace cumbersome recepts and percepts in an elegant, compact and efficient way, greatly facilitating our thinking. Dr. Bucke argues that these succinct and indirect labels, which he calls "concepts," are necessary for a conscious individual like me to be able to "stand apart from myself and contemplate myself" so I can "analyze and judge the operations of my own mind as I would analyze and judge anything else."[2] In other words, in Dr. Bucke's taxonomy, the stage of "conceptual mind" encompasses the ability to self-reflect or consciously metacognize that most— if not all—humans possess. Finally, in the stage of intuitional consciousness, there is a postulated merger of the concepts in a kind of complex union of all prior thoughts and experiences of an individual. Dr. Bucke's description of this fourth stage entails that consciousness somehow breaks free from the structure of the brain. He calls this stage "cosmic consciousness," which he describes as "a consciousness of the cosmos, that is, of the life and order of the universe."[3]

Dr. Bucke listed a number of historical characters, as well as contemporaries of his, who he believed had achieved the fourth stage, or cosmic consciousness. Some of them he extensively interviewed and studied himself. He questioned whether the experiences reported by these individuals truly reflected a *reality* perceived by them while in a higher state of consciousness, or perhaps were simply the result of a collection of hallucinations and delusions. This is a question any rational person would immediately ask. Dr. Bucke's answer to it is as sharp as it is disarming. In his own words: "We have the same evidence of the objective reality which corresponds to [cosmic consciousness] that we have of the reality which tallies any other sense or faculty whatever. Sight, for instance: You know that the tree standing there ... is real and not an hallucination, because all other persons having the sense of sight to whom you have spoken about it also see it ... Just in the same way do the reports of those who have had cosmic consciousness correspond in all essentials."[4] Indeed, all we have to assess the truthfulness of the outside world, given that we are locked inside our own heads, is the consistency of the reports we get from others about that outside world. If we apply this same litmus test to the experiences of people in a higher state of consciousness, we may be logically forced to accept the reality of those experiences on the same grounds that we accept the reality of anything else.

The work of Dr. Bucke has become one of the foundations of the field of 'transpersonal psychology,' which is defined in the *Journal of Transpersonal Psychology* as a form of psychology "concerned with the study of humanity's highest potential, and with the recognition, understanding, and realization of unitive, spiritual, and transcendent states of consciousness."[5] Myriad scientific studies can be found under the umbrella of this field, which deal with states of consciousness apparently transcending the limitations of the physical brain.

Perhaps the best-known psychiatrist to help define some of the foundations of transpersonal psychology was Dr. Carl Gustav Jung, the founder of analytical psychology. One of Dr. Jung's best-known discoveries is that of the 'collective unconscious,' derived from his work with, and observations of, schizophrenic patients.[6] The collective unconscious is regarded as a kind of reservoir of experiences of all humans—and perhaps even of other life forms—where the famous 'archetypes' of Jungian psychology reside. Every human being is believed to have access to this transpersonal repository, for which an altered state of consciousness—such as in dreams—is required. Whether or not it is necessary to attribute particular ontological reality to Dr. Jung's characterization of the collective unconscious, the empirical, clinical observations that motivated it in the first place are intriguingly suggestive of some form of consciousness that transcends the boundaries of individual human brains.

We inferred earlier that human beings like you and me should, at least in principle, be capable of accessing not only regular states of consciousness—confined to the physiology of the brain—but also boundless states akin to Dr. Bucke's cosmic consciousness. The clinical evidence supporting the principles of transpersonal psychology lend extra empirical support to this idea. If we follow this logic, it is reasonable to infer from an evolutionary perspective—just as Dr. Bucke did well over a hundred years ago—that our ability to reach the state of boundless consciousness will increase over time. Indeed, the 'fragments' of consciousness in each individual conscious being accumulate insights from information over time and 'seed' the underlying, unified field of consciousness with these insights. As this happens, the universe marches ever closer to its ultimate goal. Extrapolating this line of thought to its conclusion, we can infer that there will be a time in the cosmological future when there will no longer be a need for consciousness to be individualized; all insights of understanding and self-awareness necessary for the realization of all of consciousness' potentials will be objects in that unified consciousness. At this ultimate moment of existence, the illusion of individualization should be lifted and what Dr. Bucke called "cosmic consciousness" should become the only state of consciousness in the universe.

## Chapter 11

# God

We have surmised that the illusion of fragmentation of the original consciousness field is meant to enable the rise of self-awareness and an accumulation of self-understanding. This implies that unified consciousness was capable of *intentional* action, so to be able to cause this illusion when sufficiently motivated by certain yearnings. However, how can intentional action occur without self-reflective premeditation? After all, the original unified consciousness, as discussed earlier, was not capable of self-reflection. How could it then anticipate that the illusion of its own fragmentation would help it fulfill its desires?

The key to answering this question lies in recognizing that intentional action does not actually require self-reflective premeditation or deliberation. It can be, for lack of a better word, *instinctual*. Take ant colonies, for instance: they are capable of rather sophisticated engineering, agriculture, defense strategies, division of labor, social organization, etc. These activities are clearly intentional, in the sense that they serve well-defined purposes. Ants are even capable of adjusting their actions according to changing circumstances, so to remain on course to achieving their goals. Yet, it is difficult to imagine that ants self-reflect, in the sense of being able to introspect and turn their own intentions into objects of conscious deliberation. They do not think to the effect of saying to themselves: "Well, I have this objective, so what must I do to achieve it?" Instead, it seems safe to say that their intentionality is instinctual, arising from inborn thought templates. They simply act on their instincts, without explicit awareness of their motivations. In other words, ants clearly desire certain things, but without necessarily knowing *that* they desire.

Instinctual intentionality can conceivably be as sophisticated as self-reflective, deliberate, calculated actions, provided that the inborn thought templates are sufficiently complex. A being with complex instincts could be capable of the most sophisticated, adaptive, goal-oriented actions, though it would lack explicit awareness of its own thoughts and purposes.

I contend that highly sophisticated, inborn thought templates—archetypal in nature—have always been integral to the unified consciousness field. These complex instincts must include not only the inborn desire to realize the inherent potentials of consciousness, but also the inborn intuition of how to go about it. The exercise of these instincts, I contend, is what caused the illusion of fragmentation of consciousness.

An implication of this hypothesis is that, before there were conscious living beings in the universe, there was already a boundless, instinctual consciousness, capable of sophisticated thought patterns and driven by intent. And since this instinctual consciousness, through its intentional actions, created conscious life as we know it, we might as well call it 'God.' This way, though 'God' lacked the capacity for self-awareness due to its all-encompassing state, the breadth and depth of its instinctual vision are hard to fathom. You and I are results of the exercise of this vision.

## Chapter 12

# A natural tendency towards insight

Once you accept this instinctual drive, it follows that the same drive should translate into an *ongoing* natural tendency in the universe for each individualized consciousness to be exposed to the experiences it needs in order to accumulate the necessary insights. Anything else would defeat the original purpose and be logically inconsistent with our argument thus far. Notice that this natural tendency is something we have alluded to in an earlier chapter, and which we will explore in a little more depth here.

It is conceivable that we, as individualized consciousnesses, could choose to live our lives in a way that would shelter us from having the necessary quantitative and qualitative exposure to *experience*. This, naturally, would defeat the purpose of consciousness individualization in the first place. A subtle but inexorable tendency for each one of us to get exposure to the information necessary for an accumulation of insight would ensure the correct dynamics in the universe. Again, if you accepted, based on our earlier argumentation, that an instinctual drive could have *caused* the illusion of fragmentation of consciousness to begin with, then you must logically accept the likelihood of this natural tendency to continue on during our lives as individuals, without the need for any extra assumptions.

There is an easy—though again somewhat simplistic—analogy to help visualize this. Imagine that your existence is akin to a boat ride on a fast-flowing river. Stapp's theory entails that the 'fragment' of consciousness whose transceiver is your brain is able to make choices in your life through the collapse of the brain's wave function. These choices correspond to your ability to paddle and steer the boat in the river. However, the direction of the river's current entails a strong preferential course; in other words, an inherent and continuing natural tendency for your life to flow in certain general directions at different moments in time, exposing you to certain information and associated experiences.

Since the ultimate purpose of existence is an accumulation of the entirety of insights necessary for the completeness of universal consciousness, the choices you have made earlier in your life may naturally influence what experiences the universe will tend to bring to you later. Indeed, past choices will have influenced the experiences and associated insights that an individualized consciousness has already had, thereby altering the information that still remains to be accessed in the future.

Notice that I am *not* suggesting that each individualized consciousness has to have *all potentially* useful experiences. This would, in a way, be as inflationary as the many-worlds interpretation of quantum mechanics. Experiences are just vehicles of insight. It is conceivable that equivalent information and associated insights can be acquired with myriad different experiences, varying both quantitatively and qualitatively. This could leave some room for maneuver as far as the operation of this universal tendency towards insight is concerned, as well as room for choice as far as the individualized consciousness is concerned.

The natural tendency we are inferring here could be visualized as a law of nature that leads the material aspects of the universe to configure and arrange themselves so as to expose each individualized consciousness to the kind of experiences it needs in order to arrive at understanding. Let us thus call this tendency the 'law of insight,' for lack of a better name. Naturally, postulating such a law entails assuming the existence of yet unidentified causal influences in the material aspects of reality, through which this law could operate. Indeed, there is no other way the material universe could 'arrange itself' accordingly, as postulated above, other than through such yet unidentified causal influences. If our current scientific 'theories of everything' were sufficient to explain all of material reality in a causally-closed manner, we could immediately discard these unidentified causal influences as fallacious. But, as we have seen in Chapter 6, we cannot do it. In fact, there is much room for yet-unknown causal influences in the material world: more dimensions of space-time than we can perceive with our senses; dark matter that is not made of atoms; dark energy that we cannot detect directly; and macroscopic causal influences that may emerge as the level of complexity of systems shifts from atoms, to molecules, to tissues, to living creatures, to societies, etc., and which cannot be reduced to the properties of subatomic particles. The postulated law of insight likely operates on the basis of very large cell neighborhoods and subtle cell states, if you recall our cellular automaton analogy of the universe. In other words, the law of insight should embody a level of subtlety and range of interaction perhaps unlike most of what we know today in physics.

The subtle re-arrangement of the material world around us, as entailed by the law of insight, must logically occur in response to a gap in our understanding of nature or ourselves. A reasonable question then follows: What kind of event triggers this re-arrangement? One possibility is that the law of insight operates in reaction to our manifested thoughts and actions. On the other hand, how could a reaction to a mere thought or action represent a response to a gap in our understanding of nature? The latter seems a lot more fundamental than the former. To resolve this impasse, notice that our thoughts and actions are *always*, and *only, a reflection of our current understanding of the universe, ourselves included.* So if we say that the causal influences behind the law of insight react to our thoughts and actions, we are indirectly saying that they respond to our current understanding of nature, as originally hypothesized.

By inferring that the operation of the law of insight is

physically triggered each moment a thought or action is manifested, we are saying that it requires physical events in the brain or in the outside world to be put in motion. This is actually consistent with our line of thought, for the law of insight must be—at least partly—a *physical* law, since it needs to operate within the context of material reality. Gaps in our understanding of nature are manifested also *physically* through our neural symbol manipulations and actions. This manifestation, in turn, must *physically* trigger the unfolding of a subtle re-arrangement of the material order around us, creating suitable conditions for us to progressively eliminate those gaps.

We have to be careful though. If we assume that the law of insight somehow knows exactly what insights are still needed, then something in the universe would already have the corresponding understanding to begin with. In this case, existence would be an exercise in futility: Why would you need to contribute certain insights to unified consciousness if unified consciousness already had those insights all along? Instead, the whole point is that the necessary insights are *not* known in advance anywhere in the universe, not even by the causal mechanisms behind the law of insight. So how are these mechanisms then able to favor the right material circumstances for the acquisition of those insights?

In mathematics and computer science, the field of stochastic optimization provides a good analogy for how this may unfold. Stochastic optimization algorithms take progressive steps in the direction of finding a solution to a problem, without having any *a priori* knowledge of what the solution looks like. All that is required is the existence of a feedback mechanism that allows the algorithm to calculate whether a step taken has brought it closer, or further away, from the solution. In other words, all that is required is certain knowledge *of the problem*, not of the solution. If a step taken has made the problem worse, the algorithm can backtrack and try a step in a different direction. If, instead, the step taken has alleviated the problem, the algorithm may try a next step in the same direction. The optimization strategy does not need to entail advance knowledge of the solution in order to take correct steps towards it; it needs only to be able to iteratively evaluate the efficacy and efficiency of what it is doing at any given moment.

I submit that the law of insight operates in an analogous manner. Our thoughts and actions interact with the universe in a way that indicates, through some yet-unknown natural mechanism, how effectively and efficiently we are progressing towards greater understanding. This takes place without any *a priori* knowledge of the necessary insights. If a certain course of action or thought leads to slow progress, the natural causal influences behind the law of insight will operate to favor a change of course. Otherwise, they will operate to strengthen the current course of action or thought.

Readers familiar with optimization algorithms will have noticed that I alluded above to one of the simplest optimization strategies: a 'lazy search' algorithm. There are many other more sophisticated, effective strategies in mathematics and computer science.[1] Therefore, it is conceivable that the law of insight operates in a much more elaborate manner than suggested above. Be it as it may, it will still not know *a priori* what the particular insights are that an individualized consciousness needs. It will know simply the *directions* towards these insights.

From this we can conclude that the operation of the law of insight does not necessarily entail deliberate, self-reflective action by some knowledgeable arbitration agent. Instead, it can be a mechanistic, predictable natural tendency analogous, for instance, to magnetic attraction. As we have seen in Chapter 6, there is indeed room for such a tendency in the causal framework of material reality, at least as far as our current scientific knowledge is concerned.

# Chapter 13

# A universal memory of qualia

All life we know is limited in duration. Countless generations of presumably conscious beings have lived and died since the beginning of time. However, given that the universe is still clearly dynamic and in movement, we can safely infer that the process of universal enrichment is still underway. Therefore, countless conscious beings have passed away before the ultimate goal of existence has been achieved. If the insights they have accumulated during their lifetimes are to have contributed to the enrichment of consciousness, these insights must somehow have survived the physical existence of those conscious beings. This requires some form of memory that transcends physical structure.

As we have seen earlier, the brain operates by capturing correlations among internal symbols in neural associations. Ordinary *access* to our memories depends on an electrochemical record of these associations, the coherence of which is lost when the brain ceases to function and eventually decomposes. But understanding, as our extended Chinese Room argument illustrated, transcends mere symbol associations, residing in consciousness, not in the physical brain. As such, the possibility that presents itself to us is that there is a record of understanding in unified consciousness, which does not depend on the structure of symbol associations in the brain. This record must entail direct memory of the qualitative way an insight appears to us in consciousness—which philosophers refer to as 'qualia'—without the mediation of brain-based symbol associations. Therefore, let us call it 'memory of qualia.' Since consciousness is fundamentally boundless and unified, such memory of qualia must be a collective, universally accessible memory. Indeed, motivated by clinical observations, Jungian psychology posits something analogous. According to Jung, we all have access to a collective 'memory.'

The universal process of enrichment may then proceed as follows: each conscious being, throughout its existence, contributes certain insights of understanding to the universal memory of qualia. A record of those contributed insights survives the lifetime of any individual entity. It grows over time, becoming richer and richer in impressions, insights, understanding and self-awareness. Eventually, in a cosmological future, it may become complete.

Notice that, although there is good evidence that the symbol associations physically encoded in neural connections enable *access* to episodic memories, there is no conclusive evidence today that the information associated with these episodic memories is itself stored in the form of physical traces in the brain. However, for the sake of argument, let us assume that the brain does somehow physically store perceptual symbols. In this case, to relive an experience we must first recall information stored in physical memory. Once this information is recalled, it re-circulates through our neural networks and — because the brain operates as a transceiver of consciousness — triggers a repetition of the original conscious experience and corresponding insight. As such, there are two separate processes at play: the first process is a mere access to information, whereby stored perceptual symbols are made to circulate again across our neurons; the second process is the conscious experience that accompanies the re-circulation of these symbols. So we only relive the conscious experience at discrete times, when we choose to recall and re-circulate the corresponding information stored in physical memory. But in unified memory of qualia there can be but one process: that of conscious experience. So how can there be anything analogous to memory in it?

Think of the last major insight of understanding you had.

Try to recall that eminently self-reflective "Aha!" feeling. When you do it, you will momentarily live that experience again, but then it will go away once you shift your attention to other things. It is your brain's information storage that allows you to occasionally relive the "Aha!" experience by recalling the corresponding information. It is the fact that our brains seemingly have the capability to store information that allows us to drop certain objects from consciousness and recover them later by re-circulating the corresponding neural symbols. But in unified consciousness there is no physical information storage, so *the only way to not lose a conscious experience is to maintain it indefinitely in consciousness*. Therefore, in unified consciousness the "Aha!" feeling must be continuous, uninterrupted and permanent; it must never go away; it is never stored somewhere offline to be recalled later but, instead, must remain *ad infinitum* in consciousness. This way, 'memory' of qualia is not really memory as we normally define it, but simply *an open-ended and cumulative permanence in consciousness of every experience that has ever occurred*. Every new insight brought into unified consciousness will just add to the continuous experiencing already in it.

Let us explore this in more detail. We think of memory as a location where we can store information so we do not need to maintain our conscious attention on it; like writing something down so we can move our attention away from it. By committing something to memory we give ourselves the chance to shift our conscious focus towards something else, losing the conscious experience of what has been stored, but comfortable in the knowledge that we can replay this conscious experience any time simply by recalling the original information. We do it every time we recall images of our last vacation trip, smiling at the fond experiences this recollection allows us to relive. Using the terminology we established earlier: we store some of the precursors of neural correlates of consciousness in memory. By recalling these precursors later on and causing the corresponding symbols to re-circulate in our brains, we re-expose them to consciousness according to the transceiver model. This re-exposure allows us to subjectively re-experience the objects in consciousness corresponding to the neural correlates. Therefore, physical information memory is just a limited and indirect mechanism for reliving certain subjective experiences.

But in unified memory of qualia, by definition, there can be no neural correlates. Instead, it entails the permanence in consciousness of accumulated subjective experience. Imagine it as if you could *concurrently* hold in your consciousness every single experience you have ever had in your life, without getting tired or losing attention. This way, you could never forget anything simply because nothing would ever leave your consciousness; you would need no offline information storage for it. You would be in a state of pure, continuous and cumulative *experiencing*. It would be as if you were continuously and concurrently living every single moment of your life at once; as if all impressions and feelings you have ever had were being experienced by you now. The concept of past would lose its significance, for everything would be present. There would be no need to store something somewhere in order to recall it later, because nothing would ever leave your consciousness to begin with.

Now take your visualization one step further and imagine that you could continuously and concurrently live every single moment of the lives of every conscious being that has ever lived in the universe, at once, in a timeless fashion. This would probably get you closer to the idea of unified memory of qualia.

Once confined to a physical brain, consciousness becomes limited to the brain's ability to concurrently and continuously sustain multiple subjective experiences. This is quite logical: the apparent individualization of consciousness is achieved when it becomes restricted to the symbol manipulations occurring in the brain; that is, when consciousness can experience nothing but the symbols circulating in the brain at any moment in time. As a consequence, we cannot accumulate concurrent awareness beyond the point where the brain runs out of room to circulate extra symbols. Indeed, once the symbols corresponding to a certain subjective experience stop circulating in the brain to make room for other symbol manipulations, the original subjective experience is lost from awareness. When consciousness is confined to a physical brain, it becomes limited by the capacity of that physical brain to concurrently circulate and process multiple symbols. The ability to experience unified memory of qualia is thereby lost, at least in normal states of consciousness.

As a response to this limitation, our brains have seemingly evolved the ability to store information in physical memory, which is an indirect and constrained means for replaying certain subjective experiences. There certainly are major and obvious survival advantages to that. But—one should remember— physical information storage is only needed because an individualized consciousness becomes incapable, at least in regular states, of accessing the unified memory of qualia. Otherwise, physical information storage would be utterly unnecessary: it would be just an *indirect* and *constrained* way to achieve an effect that could already be achieved *directly* and *without constraints*.

Unified memory of qualia allows the universal process of enrichment to take place over time, in a staged, evolutionary manner. This is entirely consistent with our empirical observations of reality. After all, existence is clearly dynamic: the universe seems to be 'going somewhere,' doing something. If this 'something' is purpose-driven, as assumed, there must be a mechanism for accumulating the progress made towards its purpose over time. Otherwise, the universe would never get anywhere. There seems to be no other logical way for there to be a universal process of enrichment other than through something like universal memory of qualia.

## Chapter 14

# Interpretation and guidelines for purposeful living

In what follows, I will not try to convey a message of hope, comfort or inspiration, but simply to interpret the articulation we have built in the previous chapters. The goal is to extract rational, perhaps even inevitable conclusions from it. It so happens that these conclusions may turn out to be hopeful, comforting and perhaps even inspiring. This, of course, cannot be a bad thing. From these hopeful conclusions, if so desired, we will be able to logically derive some guidelines for optimizing the way we live our lives along the lines of purpose and meaning.

There is much meaning to your life right now, independently of the lives of others, to the extent that the experiences you go through in your life expose you to new insights of understanding. Through your experiences as an individualized consciousness, the universe goes a step further in understanding itself and becomes more self-aware. Even the feelings of confusion, disorientation and loss are but logical precursors of greater understanding. Every minute you live, every experience you go through, pleasant or not, rewarding or not, painful or not, contributes to the ultimate universal goal of understanding and self-awareness. There is meaning in your life whether you see and understand it or not; whether you enjoy your life or not; whether you feel miserable or exultant; whether you are healthy or terminally ill; whether you live in community or alone; whether your life is long or short. The reason this rich meaning is often not obvious to you is the fact that your consciousness is confined to the indirect and limited models of reality in your brain. This necessary illusion aside, the meaning of your life is a constant, a certainty, regardless of the choices you make or the circumstances you face. All circumstances of your life are but vehicles of experience and understanding, favored in subtle ways by the law of insight.

That said, choices also have a meaning and a purpose. The choices you make can help increase the efficacy and efficiency of the universal journey towards insight and self-awareness. The articulation in this book cannot provide guidance regarding what insights or experiences each one of us needs to have; from a rational perspective, these remain a mystery. But your choices in life will logically define how effectively and efficiently you will have those necessary insights, thereby contributing to universal completeness.

By the same token, your choices may also slow down your progress towards insight. It is conceivable that your consciousness may register the natural consequences of this slowing down as pain and suffering, for pain and suffering are known to be very effective in getting people to re-think their choices and open their minds to new thoughts and perspectives. From this point of view, pain and suffering are likely instruments of the material causal mechanisms leveraged by the law of insight.

As stated earlier, these interpretations lead us to the conclusion that our lives have meaning in and by themselves. In fact, regardless of how inert, sterile, senseless and futile one's life may feel like, there are always a few modest steps being contributed to the greater universal purpose, even if one is not at all aware of it. Indeed, the very feelings of stagnation and futility are experiences in themselves. Just by being conscious and alive we must already be making a contribution.

What about the lives of others? One interesting consequence of our conclusions is that, at the most fundamental level of existence, other living beings are simply other versions of yourself; you and they are all but different manifestations of the same unified consciousness field. In a quite fundamental way, by observing others you are but learning about yourself;

a nice thought to have next time somebody pisses you off. In a way, others mirror your own characteristics for the benefit of your observation and learning, while you mirror theirs for their learning.

Like us, each of our fellow human beings — in fact, each sentient entity in the universe — is contributing to the same universal goal. From a universal perspective, insights contributed to unified consciousness by you or by other conscious entities are equally necessary to the end purpose and, in that sense, equivalent. Therefore, reaching new insights yourself and helping other conscious entities to do so are equivalent contributions to the enrichment of the universe.

It is thus logical that, if you want to live as effective and efficient a life as possible, as far as contributing to the ultimate universal goal is concerned, you may do well not only to try and reach as many insights as possible yourself, but also to contribute to the ability of others to learn and reach their insights as well. Through helping others to reach understanding, you would be multiplying the efficacy and efficiency of your own life many fold. In this case, it is reasonable to expect that the postulated law of insight will causally influence the circumstances surrounding your life to optimize your ability to continue to do so. This natural tendency will lead to a re-arrangement of material reality around you, in conformity with the known laws of physics plus some other causal influences that we have not yet discovered scientifically.

Naturally, this is a complex optimization problem. Hypothetically, by trying to optimize your ability to help others the law of insight could end up reducing your ability to reach insights yourself. As a matter of fact, if everybody were busy helping others to reach insights, but neglecting their own need for understanding, nobody would ever get anywhere and all this help would be fruitless. This way, the law of insight may be configured to hit a subtle sweet spot of maximum compound efficacy and efficiency, the sense of which may be incomprehensible to our brains' limited capacity to build models of reality. In other words, it is reasonable to expect that you will often not understand why the universe is influencing your life the way it does.

Similarly, when your choices and actions interfere with the ability of others to arrive effectively and efficiently at the understandings they need, it is reasonable to expect that the postulated law of insight will causally influence the circumstances surrounding your life to minimize your ability to continue to do so. In addition, since the very action of negatively interfering with the progress of others will likely reflect a gap in your understanding of nature, it is also reasonable to expect that the law of insight will favor certain—potentially painful—experiences in your life to help you cover that gap. Again, all of this would have to take place in the context of a large compound optimization problem, which will very likely exceed the capacity of the human brain to correctly model and interpret.

This optimization problem is yet further compounded when one logically contemplates the possibility that our lives may *also* serve as tools for the learning of others. The way others perceive your behavior, experiences, emotions and general situation may be a valuable instrument for their own insights. This is particularly so when it comes to people who care about you or upon whom you hold influence. From this, one can imagine that even someone in a deep state of coma still serves the purpose of enabling certain experiences and insights for his or her loved ones, care-givers, etc., just by remaining alive. Insofar as there may be tendencies in our lives arising for the sake of the insights of others, we may indeed be living under the subtle influence of an astonishingly complex but ultimately natural, positive, meaningful and ever-present optimization mechanism.

A question that arises at this point is: If you want to multiply the efficacy and efficiency of your existence by helping others accumulate understanding, how can you go about it? After all, as noted earlier, we have no rational guidelines for guessing which experiences we or other individuals require. We just do not know; nobody knows. The best we can hope for is that the law of insight will help bring the necessary experiences to us and others, while maintaining an attitude of openness towards the results of its operation. So if I cannot know what my neighbors need to experience, how can I help them? As a matter of fact, if I do not know what *I* need, how can I help myself to lead an effective and efficient life? There are a few reasonable inferences we can still make here.

Even though we cannot know what experiences we or others require, *we know that we all require a variety of experiences.* After all, this is the whole point of living. There are a few basic conditions that surely help us all have as many experiences as possible: healthy bodies and minds to go places and do things; education to aid true understanding of the things we experience; communion with others, so we can exchange and debate ideas and feelings, observing one another, thereby enriching our understanding of ourselves and others; etc. Helping others achieve these basic conditions seems like a safe and solid way to help universal enrichment along.

Regarding your own self, the greatest potential impediments to the efficacy and efficiency of your own existence seem to be lack of curiosity and critical thinking, apathy, procrastination and a type of unreasonable fear that may stop you from chasing after the experiences you aspire to have. Even failure, disaster and disease that happen upon you without your choosing may give you intense and immensely worthwhile experiences. They may ultimately end your life but not before giving you, and others who care about you, powerful new perspectives the universe may have needed to experience. Whereas procrastination is perhaps mostly a waste of time and energy, a life proactively devoted to exploration, investigation, (self-) discovery, intense and varied experiences, adventure, communion with others, charity, contribution, constructive achievements, self-development, etc., would very likely be in profound harmony with the ultimate universal purpose.

We briefly touched above on the subject of disease and physical death. What conclusions regarding death can we extract from our articulation? Before addressing this, we need to briefly define what it means to be you, since death is supposedly about the end of you. As we have inferred earlier, all you have ever felt, thought or perceived in your entire life has been no more than subjective objects in your consciousness. Even your perception of your own body has been but an object in your consciousness. Your physical brain and body have been just tools of your consciousness: a highly sophisticated, semi-autonomous transceiver with sensors and actuators, so to speak. They could be interpreted, according to our articulation, as somewhat analogous to your clothes, car, spectacles or any other tool you may have used to interact with the material aspects of reality. From this perspective, your body is not you; you are just its user. With your body and brain outside of the picture, what you recognize as being you is basically a collection of experiences; that is, feelings, insights and impressions. There is nothing more that could be you. These experiences have a coherent history, which gives you a notion of who or what you are in relation to who or what you are not.

Since you are a manifestation of a unified consciousness, this entire collection of experiences with which you identify yourself must be, by default, forever preserved in the universal memory of qualia. Therefore, there is nothing about who or what you are that is lost upon the loss of coherence of your physical body; at least nothing fundamentally more than what is lost if you, for instance, throw some old clothes away.

If this idea does not sink in at first, think about it for a moment. There is nothing you can identify yourself with other than objects in your own consciousness, whatever these objects are. Whatever else there may exist in the universe that has never been an object in your consciousness might as well never have existed, as far as you are concerned. So you cannot possibly identify yourself with it. Now, since every object that has ever been in your consciousness is inferred to stay in unified consciousness as a permanent experience—recall the 'universal memory of qualia'—then there can never be anything about you, any aspect or property of you, that can ever be lost at a universal scale. The very subjective experience of being you, with all that it entails, including all the feelings, impressions and insights that you are having right now, as you read this, can never be lost.

Even if you rationally accept the above, you may still have a nagging feeling that something will change or be lost; that you will somehow not be quite yourself upon physical death. However, if you accept our argumentation up to this point, the very opposite must the true. Indeed, can you remember what it was like to be you when you were a baby or a toddler? Can you relive in your mind, with all its richness, textures and nuances, the sweetness and lightness of being a child? Can you remember and subjectively relive every intense experience you ever had in your life? Every moment, every person that made a mark on you as an individual? Probably not. Yet, all these feelings and perceptions are an inherent part of what it is to be you. In a certain way, you are not quite a complete version of yourself right now. But if your consciousness were to reach a state wherein all those feelings and perceptions would return and be relived at once, concurrently and continuously, you would be more *you* than ever before.

If your consciousness returns fully to its underlying boundless state, you will also be everybody else to the same extent that you will be more yourself. So there is no loss, but only an addition; and what an addition. Yet, you will obviously part with your ego, for without the constraints imposed by a physical brain your consciousness will lose the foreground/background framework that gives you a separate identity. From this perspective, it is entirely logical to state, without any contradiction, that physical death may entail the lifting of the illusion of your individuality, or ego, without the loss of anything that has something to do with the experience of being you.

Another intriguing consequence of this line of thought is this: once returned to its boundless state, thereby regaining access to the universal memory of qualia, your consciousness will likely be able to come in more intimate contact with other individualized 'fragments' of consciousness than ever possible when confined to a physical brain. These other individualized 'fragments' of consciousness could be those of living people as well as of people who have already passed away. After all, we have inferred that all past is present at the level of universal memory of qualia. In fact, to describe this as 'intimate contact' is an understatement: it must be more like *being* the other person, in every way that it means something to be another person while still being you. There can be no higher or more intense proximity or intimacy conceivable.

It is inescapable to conclude from our argument that nobody ever truly dies and nobody is ever truly lost to others. Life is not ephemeral, as feared by Kundera. In fact, Nietzsche's 'eternal return'—the idea that everything that has ever happened will happen again, and again—seems to be true in the only way that really counts: the eternity of our subjective experiences.

Perhaps the most significant question in all this is the following: Do you need to physically pass away in order to regain the state of boundless consciousness? The psychiatric investigations of Dr. Bucke, which we reviewed earlier, suggest that human beings can reach analogous states of consciousness while physically alive. His investigations, along with the reported experiences of people like Dr. Taylor during her brain stroke, also suggest that there are several degrees to which we can reach that expanded state of consciousness. To me, this is one of the most intriguing and fascinating topics of investigation and self-development.

Rationality and the pursuit of spirituality do not need to be mutually exclusive. All one needs is an adherence to what is perhaps the most important—and most often forgotten—principle of science: know what you do not know and keep an open mind. Indeed, rationality and logic may be fundamental tools to spirituality, for they allow us to make inferences about things that we may not (yet) be able to verify either objectively or subjectively.

This book is not science. But it is, hopefully, logical, coherent in articulation and not inconsistent with established scientific fact. All too often, rational people are put off from the pursuit of spirituality because their minds cannot tolerate the apparent inconsistencies and seemingly unfounded assumptions that are often associated with spirituality. Because of this huge and often justifiable mental barrier, these rational people are unable to complement their objective assessment and knowledge of nature with their crucial counterparts: *subjective* assessment and knowledge of nature. They simply do not allow themselves the mental freedom to do it because their rationality forces them to dismiss crucial steps along the path of subjective exploration. This is a modern human tragedy, disproportionally affecting the most educated and intelligent segments of society.

Given that you were obviously attracted to the title of this book, you are probably one of the educated, intelligent, rational people I spoke of above. It is my sincere wish that this book has helped you break from your initial preconceptions, so that your rational mind can allow you a little more latitude to investigate spiritual ideas.

I want to leave you with a final thought in this chapter. As a rational, critical person, you may be keenly aware of how your mind can play tricks on you; anything from optical illusions to full-blown hallucinations. Because of this, you may often tend to question and doubt the reliability of your own conscious impressions, particularly when it comes to higher states of consciousness. This is a healthy attitude, as long as it does not make you throw away the baby with the bath water. For ultimately, whether you trust or mistrust the impressions in it, *all you have is your own consciousness.*

## Chapter 15

# Related concepts

I have tried to construct a coherent argument about the ultimate purpose of existence. The argument comprises a series of inferences connected by a logical thread. Many of these inferences, which arise naturally from the logic of the argument, entail aspects of reality that transcend the scope of scientific verification. Yet, many of those aspects have already been proposed and debated since remote antiquity in philosophical and spiritual circles, and I make no claims of originality about proposing them. It is the overall coherent argument that I hope to be the key contribution of this book. That said, the fact that much of what has been inferred here turns out to correspond well to philosophical and spiritual ideas proposed by many others, throughout history, provides a degree of reassurance and confidence about these inferences.

In what follows, I will briefly touch upon philosophical and spiritual ideas that strongly resemble conclusions of this book. You may do more research on these ideas yourself, so to gain more insight into how they fit within the logical framework laid out in previous chapters. However, notice that I am not necessarily endorsing the ideas described below in the form that they may have been described elsewhere. In fact, the argument built in earlier chapters does not support certain interpretations of these ideas or features attributed to them. Whichever the case, my argument and position are limited to what has been discussed in the previous chapters, the references below being provided merely for further information. The list below is certainly not complete, which reflects gaps in my familiarity with spiritual literature rather than a veiled attempt to imply unwarranted originality for my work.

Having made the necessary disclaimers, let us get on with it. We have built our argument on the idea that our individual, self-reflective consciousness is immaterial. We have also posited that the material universe, including our own physical bodies, is an experiential manifestation of an obfuscated mind that extends far beyond our own individual consciousness, and with which we interact. This is related to the age-old concept of mind/body dualism. Ancient Iranian prophet and poet Zoroaster already wrote about dualism thousands of years ago. Later, Greek philosophers Plato and Aristotle spoke of the existence of an immaterial soul, which is perhaps somewhat analogous to the immaterial consciousness of our argument. In the seventeenth century, the idea of dualism was elaborated upon by René Descartes, as alluded to in a previous chapter. To this day, dualism is a very influential idea in philosophical discourse, particularly in the field of philosophy of mind.

The justification we used to assert that consciousness is irreducible to matter was two-fold: Wigner's interpretation of quantum physics; and the philosophical argument that we have no direct access to a material world allegedly outside consciousness. These arguments entail that consciousness—mentality—has primacy over material existence, which is not a novel concept. Many authors, particularly since the early twentieth century, have argued that consciousness is the ground of all existence. Notable early work on this was done by Alfred North Whitehead.[1] More modern authors include Peter Russell[2] and Amit Goswami.[3] Russell adopts a more philosophical perspective, while Goswami explores a more physics-oriented interpretation of the role of consciousness.

The law of insight postulated earlier is related to the 'law of karma' of many Eastern spiritual traditions, as well as to the Judeo-Christian tenet that we 'reap what we sow.' From this perspective, the so-called 'karma' would, in principle, not be related to punishment/reward, debit/credit or any other reflection of anthropomorphic morality. Instead, it would simply be a morally neutral, natural tendency operating at a significant level of sophistication and subtlety.

Finally, the idea of a universal memory of qualia is somewhat related to the mystical concept of 'Akashic records.' The Akashic records are postulated to be a non-physical, universal 'filing system' of all human experience, as well as the experiences of other conscious entities. Mystics believe that humans can access the Akashic records through altered states of consciousness, thereby gaining knowledge otherwise impossible to reach through ordinary physical means. In the Judeo-Christian tradition, the idea of a universal memory of qualia may bear some resemblance to the 'Book of Life,' where God records the lives of human beings.

When I set out to write this book, I knew that some of the ideas I would touch upon were very similar to concepts mystics and religious people have talked about for centuries. A form of dualism was one such an idea. However, as I begun constructing the argument for a rationalist spirituality, a few other ideas begun to emerge that were remarkably close to yet other mystical and spiritual concepts. For instance, I had not conceived of all implications and nuances of a universal memory of qualia until a relatively late stage of writing. Indeed, analyzing the partial argument I had written down up until that point, it dawned on me that something with the full power of the universal memory of qualia was necessary to logically close the argument. Sure enough, there was something in religious and esoteric literature that was eerily similar to that. This experience recurred a few more times, as I continued writing.

So I was left in a curious frame of mind. The old scriptures where those mystical and religious ideas appeared for the first time were not logically inferred, but cast as revelation. Could it be that there is a more direct and clearer way to gain access to the most profound truths of nature other than through logical, rational inquiry? Could it be that Dr. Bucke's state of cosmic consciousness could reveal the way nature works in a manner that completely bypasses the often laborious and unreliable manipulation of neural symbols in the brain?

If these speculations are true, this book has been merely the result of a tortuous, indirect intellectual exercise that would not have been necessary if you and I had achieved cosmic consciousness. Perhaps the conclusions extracted here are but partial, blurred, shimmering shadows of a much more complete and nuanced truth. Standing where I am now, with this book completed before me, I intuit that this is but the tentative beginning of a much longer journey.

# Endnotes

## Chapter 1
1   Richard P. Feynman, "The Pleasure of Finding Things Out", Perseus Publishing, Cambridge, Massachusetts, 1999, pp. 24-25.
2   Daniel Dennett, "Cute, sexy, sweet, funny", a talk given at TED conference, February 2009.

## Chapter 2
1   Milan Kundera, "The Unbearable Lightness of Being", Harper & Row, 1984, p. 8.

## Chapter 3
1   Some might argue that, instead, the universe might *be comprised* in the complete entity. This may be a valid assertion under a different definition of 'universe' but, in this book, the words 'universe' and 'nature' are each meant to encompass both Creation and potential Creator. This is not, in any way, an attempt to dismiss the power or importance of the concept of a Supreme Being, but simply a semantic necessity to keep my discourse short and consistent.

## Chapter 4
1   See, for instance: Ran R. Hassin, editor, "The New Unconscious", Oxford Series in Social Cognition and Social Neuroscience, Oxford University Press, USA, October 2004.
2   David J. Chalmers, "The Conscious Mind: In Search of a Fundamental Theory", Oxford University Press, 1996.
3   See, for instance: Joseph Levine, "Conceivability, Identity, and the Explanatory Gap", in: Stuart R. Hameroff, Alfred W. Kaszniak, and David J. Chalmers, editors, "Toward a Science of Consciousness III, The Third Tucson Discussions

and Debates", October 1999. See also: Joseph Levine, "Materialism and Qualia: The Explanatory Gap", Pacific Philosophical Quarterly 64, 1983, pp. 354-361.

4   See, for instance: Francis Crick and Christof Koch, "Towards a neurobiological theory of consciousness", Seminars in Neuroscience 2, 1990, pp. 263–275.

5   Kurzweil's position is extensively elaborated upon in: Ray Kurzweil, "The Singularity Is Near: When Humans Transcend Biology", Viking, 2005, pp. 458-469, where Kurzweil counters John Searle's "Chinese Room" argument with the complexity and emergentist hypothesis.

6   Rodney Brooks, Ray Kurzweil, and David Gelernter, "Will Machines Become Conscious? Gelernter, Kurzweil debate machine consciousness", a debate held at MIT in November 2006, with an online transcript available at http://www.kurzweilai.net.

7   Steve Kotler, interviewer, "The Neurology of Spiritual Experience", h+ magazine, digital edition, fall of 2009, p. 45.

8   Erich Joos, "The Emergence of Classicality from Quantum Theory", in: Philip Clayton and Paul Davies, editors, "The Re-Emergence of Emergence: The Emergentist Hypothesis from Science to Religion", Oxford University Press, 2006, pp. 53-78.

## Chapter 5

1   See, for instance: Thomas Metzinger, editor, "Neural Correlates of Consciousness: Empirical and Conceptual Questions", The MIT Press, September 2000.

2   See, for instance: Ray B. Smith, "Cranial Electrotherapy Stimulation: Its First Fifty Years, Plus Three: A Monograph", Tate Publishing & Enterprises, March 2008.

3   See, for instance: M.T. Alkire and J. Miller, "General anesthesia and the neural correlates of consciousness", Progress in Brain Research 150, 2005, pp. 229-244.

4   See, for instance: Steve Squyres, "Roving Mars: Spirit, Opportunity, and the Exploration of the Red Planet", Hyperion, January 2007.

5   For an extensive review of related studies, see: Jeffrey M. Schwartz and Sharon Begley, "The Mind and the Brain: Neuroplasticity and the Power of Mental Force", Harper Collins, New York, 2002.

6   Jeffrey M. Schwartz, Henry P. Stapp, and Mario Beauregard, "Quantum physics in neuroscience and psychology: a neurophysical model of mind–brain interaction", Philosophical Transactions of the Royal Society B, doi:10.1098/rstb.2004.1598, 2005, p. 3.

7   Penrose's original work on this is: Roger Penrose, "The Emperor's New Mind", Oxford University Press, 1989. He elaborated further in: Roger Penrose, "Shadows of the Mind: A Search for the Missing Science of Consciousness", Vintage, 1995. His ideas were summarized and debated with other scientists in: Roger Penrose, Abner Shimony, Nancy Cartwright, and Stephen Hawking, "The Large, the Small, and the Human Mind", Cambridge University Press, 1997.

8   See, for instance: Stuart Hameroff, "Consciousness, neurobiology and quantum mechanics: The case for a connection", in: Jack A. Tuszynski, editor, "The Emerging Physics of Consciousness" (The Frontiers Collection), Springer, 2006, pp. 193-242.

9   An excellent and accessible volume elaborating on Stapp's ideas is: Henry P. Stapp, "Mindful Universe: Quantum Mechanics and the Participating Observer" (The Frontiers Collection), Springer, 2007. A more technical one is: Henry P. Stapp, "Mind, Matter and Quantum Mechanics" (The Frontiers Collection), Springer, 2003.

## Chapter 6

1   For an extensive and accessible overview, see: Iain Nicolson,

"Dark Side of the Universe: Dark Matter, Dark Energy, and the Fate of the Universe", Canopus Publishing Limited, 2007.

2    An excellent and accessible resource about string theories and M-theory is: Brian Greene, "The Elegant Universe: Superstrings, Hidden Dimensions and the Quest for the Ultimate Theory", Vintage, 2005.

3    Mile Gu, Christian Weedbrook, Alvaro Perales, and Michael A. Nielsen, "More Really is Different", arXiv:0809.0151v1 [cond-mat.other], August 2008, p. 1.

4    Robert B. Laughlin and David Pines, "The Theory of Everything", Proceedings of the National Academy of Sciences 97(1), January 2000, p. 28.

5    See Zuse's seminal book: Konrad Zuse,"*Rechnender Raum*", Friedrich Vieweg & Sohn, 1969.

6    One of the first and best known experiments showing instantaneous interaction at a distance has been reported in: Alain Aspect *et al.*, "Experimental Tests of Realistic Local Theories via Bell's Theorem", Physical Review Letters 47, 460, 1981. Since then, many other experiments have been performed, confirming Aspect's conclusions. The most recent experiment, at the time this book was written, had been reported in: D. Salart *et al.*, "Space-like Separation in a Bell Test Assuming Gravitationally Induced Collapses", Physical Review Letters 100, 220404, 2008.

7    P.W. Anderson, "More Is Different", Science, New Series, Vol. 177, No. 4047, August 4, 1972, pp. 393-396.

8    Mile Gu *et al.*, *op. cit.*.

## Chapter 7

1    The thought experiment has been described here: John R. Searle, "Minds, brains, and programs", Behavioral and Brain Sciences 3 (3), 1980, pp. 417-457.

2    John R. Searle, *op. cit.*, p. 419.

3   Their project has been described in the following article: Henry Markram, "The Blue Brain Project", Nature Reviews Neuroscience 7, February 2006, pp. 153-160.

4   Henry Markram, "Henry Markram builds a brain in a supercomputer", a talk given at TEDGlobal conference, July 2009.

5   Henry Markram, *op. cit.*, 2009.

6   An excellent and very accessible overview of Haikonen's ideas can be found in: Pentti O. Haikonen, "The Cognitive Approach to Conscious Machines", Imprint Academic, March 2003.

7   Randall O'Reilly and Yuko Munakata, "Computational Explorations in Cognitive Neuroscience: Understanding the Mind by Simulating the Brain", MIT Press, September 2000.

## Chapter 8

1   Claude E. Shannon, "A Mathematical Theory of Communication", Bell System Technical Journal, volume 27, July, October, 1948, pp. 379-423, 623-656.

2   Claude E. Shannon, *op. cit.*, p. 379.

3   Zeno's paradoxes are a set of problems devised by Zeno of Elea, a pre-Socratic Greek philosopher of southern Italy. The paradox of "Achilles and the tortoise" is one of Zeno's eight surviving paradoxes. It goes as follows: in a race where the tortoise has a head start, it is stated that Achilles can never overtake the tortoise, even though he can run much faster. The idea is that, in order to overtake the tortoise, Achilles has first to cover the distance that initially separated him from the tortoise. In the time it takes him to do so, the tortoise will have moved a short distance further, and still be ahead of Achilles. Achilles then has to cover *that* short distance but, by the time he does so, the tortoise will again be a little further, and so on. So Achilles can never overtake the tortoise, which, of course, contradicts observation. Naturally, this

is only a paradox if we assume that an infinite number of steps requires infinite time to be performed. In practice, however, the time taken by each subsequent step becomes increasingly shorter. Therefore, even though Achilles does need an infinite number of steps to overtake the tortoise, he performs those steps in finite time.

4    Jill Bolte Taylor, "Jill Bolte Taylor's stroke of insight", a talk given at TED conference, 2008.

5    Cosimo Urgesi, Salvatore M. Aglioti, Miran Skrap, and Franco Fabbro, "The Spiritual Brain: Selective Cortical Lesions Modulate Human Self-Transcendence", Neuron 65, February 11, 2010, pp. 309-319.

6    Aldous Huxley, "The Doors of Perception and Heaven and Hell", Vintage Books, London, 2004, pp. 10-11.

## Chapter 10

1    Richard Maurice Bucke, editor, "Cosmic Consciousness: A Study in the Evolution of the Human Mind", Innes & Sons, Philadelphia, 1905.

2    Richard Maurice Bucke, *op. cit.*, p. 14.

3    Richard Maurice Bucke, *op. cit.*, p. 2.

4    Richard Maurice Bucke, *op. cit.*, p. 59.

5    D.H. Lajoie and S.I. Shapiro, "Definitions of transpersonal psychology: The first twenty-three years", Journal of Transpersonal Psychology, Vol. 24, 1992, p. 91.

6    The use of the qualifier 'unconscious' does not imply that the contents of the collective unconscious are outside consciousness itself, but only beyond the reach of ordinary, self-reflective introspection.

## Chapter 12

1    See, for instance: James C. Spall, "Introduction to Stochastic Search and Optimization", Wiley-Interscience, March 2003.

# Chapter 15

1   See, for instance: Alfred North Whitehead, "Adventures of Ideas", The Macmillan Company, New York, 1933.

2   See, for instance: Peter Russell, "From Science to God: A Physicist's Journey into the Mystery of Consciousness", New World Library, March 2003.

3   A largely self-contained overview of Amit Goswami's ideas on consciousness can be found in: Amit Goswami with Richard E. Reed and Maggie Goswami, "The Self-Aware Universe: How Consciousness Creates the Material World", Jeremy P. Tarcher/Putman, New York, 1993.

**BOOKS**

## ACADEMIC AND SPECIALIST

Iff Books publishes non-fiction. It aims to work with authors and titles that augment our understanding of the human condition, society and civilisation, and the world or universe in which we live.
If you have enjoyed this book, why not tell other readers by posting a review on your preferred book site.
Recent bestsellers from Iff Books are:

### The Fall
Steve Taylor
*The Fall* discusses human achievement versus the issues of war, patriarchy and social inequality.
Paperback: 978-1-90504-720-8 ebook: 978-184694-633-2

### Framespotting
Changing How You Look at Things Changes How
You See Them
Laurence & Alison Matthews
A punchy, upbeat guide to framespotting. Spot deceptions and hidden assumptions; swap growth for growing up. See and be free.
Paperback: 978-1-78279-689-3 ebook: 978-1-78279-822-4

## Is There an Afterlife?
David Fontana
Is there an Afterlife? If so what is it like? How do Western ideas
of the afterlife compare with Eastern? David Fontana presents
the historical and contemporary evidence for survival of physical
death.
Paperback: 978-1-90381-690-5

## Nothing Matters
A Book About Nothing
Ronald Green
Thinking about Nothing opens the world to everything by
illuminating new angles to old problems and stimulating new
ways of thinking.
Paperback: 978-1-84694-707-0 ebook: 978-1-78099-016-3

## Panpsychism
The Philosophy of the Sensuous Cosmos
Peter Ells
Are free will and mind chimeras? This book, anti-materialistic
but respecting science, answers: No! Mind is foundational to all
existence.
Paperback: 978-1-84694-505-2 ebook: 978-1-78099-018-7

Readers of ebooks can buy or view any of these bestsellers by
clicking on the live link in the title. Most titles are published in
paperback and as an ebook. Paperbacks are available in traditional
bookshops. Both print and ebook formats are available online.
Find more titles and sign up to our readers' newsletter at http://
www.johnhuntpublishing.com/non-fiction
Follow us on Facebook at https://www.facebook.com/
JHPNonFiction
and Twitter at https://twitter.com/JHPNonFiction